W9-ABZ-361

ROY FULLER

A TRIBUTE

ROY FULLER

A TRIBUTE

Edited by
A.T. Tolley

Carleton University Press
Ottawa, Canada
1993

PR
6011
.U5
Z8
1993

©Carleton University Press Inc. 1993

ISBN   0-88629-211-5 (paperback)
ISBN   0-88629-210-7 (casebound)

Printed and bound in Canada

Carleton General List

Canadian Cataloguing in Publication Data
Main entry under title:

   Roy Fuller : a tribute

Includes bibliographical references.

ISBN 0-88629-210-7 (bound)
ISBN 0-88629-211-5 (pbk.)

1. Fuller, Roy, 1912–1991–Criticism and interpretation.   2. Fuller,
Roy, 1912–1991–Biography.   I. Tolley, A.T.

PR6011.U55Z92 1993   821'.914   C93-090186-X

Distributed by   Oxford University Press Canada,
                 70 Wynford Drive,
                 Don Mills, Ontario,
                 Canada. M3C 1J9
                 (416) 441-2941

Cover design: Chris Jackson

Acknowledgements

Carleton University Press gratefully acknowledges the support extended to its publishing programme by the Canada Council and the
Ontario Arts Council.

The Press would also like to thank the Department of Communi-
cations, Government of Canada, and the Government of Ontario
through the Ministry of Culture, Tourism and Recreation, for their
assistance.

2 802 4392

To Hazel

poetic creator of
Leily, Begam, Dozey, Mrs. Elbow
and Jarman-Jarman

Other books by A.T. Tolley

The Early Poetry of Stephen Spender: A Chronology
The Poetry of the Thirties
The Poetry of the Forties
My Proper Ground: A Study of the Work of Philip Larkin and its Development

Edited by A.T. Tolley

John Lehmann: A Tribute

Contents

Acknowledgements

My first debt is to the contributors to this volume, who cheerfully wrote their best without prospect of fee. I have to thank especially John Fuller, who has assisted with suggestions, criticisms and other help almost from the start. He provided the poem by Roy Fuller with which this book opens, and gave permission for its inclusion, as well as for the use of quotations from Roy Fuller's work.

I should also like to thank Michael Gnarowski of Carleton University Press for his support and confidence, without which I could not have set out to bring together this volume.

For my own contributions, I have to thank Christopher Sheppard and his staff at the Brotherton Collection at the University of Leeds for their valuable and courteous assistance in my consultation of Roy Fuller's notebooks; and the University of Leeds and the Estate of Roy Fuller for allowing me to quote from the notebooks. John Fuller brought to my attention items I was not aware of in compiling the bibliography; and Steven Smith kindly provided information that he had gathered for the descriptive bibliography of Roy Fuller's work that he was preparing.

My work was done with the support of a grant from the Social Sciences and Humanities Research Council of Canada. The Dean of Graduate Studies and Research at Carleton University made a generous grant towards the preparing of the text.

My wife Glenda gave valuable editorial comment and also kindly typed most of the book.

ROY FULLER

Duke in Exile

The Duke in exile, trying to escape
From folly's times that fail even to serve
The fools.
          Along the woodland ride observes
Contiguous, almost circular patterns where
The horseman passed; and thanks his stars he is
Unalterable in his cowardice.
Forsythia buds hang like a ripe sow's teats —
It's only just philosophizing weather;
Putting great questions underneath the sky.

Wed to a beggar, how is it to end
In the princess's favour ? Even if
The spouse were to expire, and thus allow
A marriage to a king, she would have been
Spoilt irretrievably in royal eyes.
It must be that the smelly, ragged fellow
Turns out to be a prince, bewitched; or, like
The Duke himself, testing the pastoral,
The erring or virtuous subjects of his realm.

A warning: buy no gallows flesh, nor sit
At the edge of any well. But who'd pursue
Either bizarre activity? Yet we
May push a door and find a dear one hanging,
Before a nightmare fall into the depths.

There's always a season for unhappiness,
Appropriate or not. The festivals
Of piety or husbandry mark out
The months of pain. His duchess sorely ailed
When the March moon was at its slenderest,
And as his jester went on making jokes.

Still does. But while the greater clowns intrigue
For federated power to start the wars
That will go on until the world is dead,
The ducal clown is consciously a clown;
Knowing of Ovid's exile among the Goths,
Chooses the powerless arboreal court
Where even an equally impuissant sun
Compels the honey-bees, if not mankind,
From still exiguous blossoming begin
A harmless social order once again.

Introduction

Among readers of poetry, the work of Roy Fuller is widely admired and loved. Among those whose knowledge of twentieth-century English poetry is comprehensive and discriminating, his writing is highly esteemed. The occasion of this book is a sad one: it is offered as a token of valedictory respect on the passing of a major talent. Yet it is hoped that the book will have a purpose beyond this — that it will illuminate Roy Fuller's achievement and establish more firmly a public recognition of his place in English poetry of this century.

A poet who never caught on: that is the way that Fuller purported to see himself in recent years, after a career that had produced some sixteen major collections of poetry and that included being Oxford Professor of Poetry and receiving the Queen's Gold Medal for Poetry and a C.B.E. What "catching on" amounts to in these days is a little open to question. Very few poets attain the popularity of Betjeman or Larkin. Many sell well, like Eliot, after they are dead and have come to be admitted to the canon of English poetry — or, more importantly, to the syllabus of English-language schools. Dylan Thomas might be said to be a poet who caught on — as did Alan Ginsberg in America: culture heroes in their lifetimes. Auden, Spender, Day Lewis and MacNeice "caught on" in the left-wing literary movement of the thirties; though their readership was much greater during World War II. The poets associated with the Movement, other than Larkin, may also be said to have caught the literary limelight — at least for quite a time. What then was the case with Roy Fuller; who, as he related himself, found it difficult, in his late years, to find someone to publish his prize-winning masterpiece, *Available for Dreams* (1989) — one of the outstanding collections of poetry to appear in the last fifty years?

It was not that Fuller's poetry was brought out in obscurity, like R.S. Thomas's outstanding first volumes, which were published in mid-Wales in the forties. His work was early taken up by John Lehmann, then an editor of power, who published Fuller's poetry in *New Writing* and *Penguin New Writing* and from the Hogarth Press and from his own publishing house. It seems rather that Fuller came along at the wrong time. As Lehmann once said to me, he was a sort of "thirties poet who came along a bit later". Julian Symons has recounted how he started *Twentieth Century Verse* in 1937 to provide an outlet for poets whose work seemed to have difficulty in making its way in a literary ethos that had come to be dominated by Auden and his associates; and Fuller's first volume, *Poems* (1939), appeared as one of the Fortune Poets series initiated by Symons. By the time he was taken up by Lehmann, the poetry of social realism associated with the Left in the 'thirties was out of fashion; and, while Fuller served in the Fleet Air Arm, he never saw action, and his very fine second and third volumes, *The Middle of a War* (1942) and *A Lost Season* (1944), did not qualify him as the war poet that British readers were looking for. When he came out of the Navy, he emerged in a world in which his lingering respect for "Uncle Joe" Stalin seemed increasingly anachronistic. I remember him telling a bemused meeting of the Oxford English Club in 1949 that all poetry was in a sense political — a view for which the audience had not been prepared by their almost universal admiration of Dylan Thomas's *Deaths and Entrances*. Indeed, one senses, in Fuller's two immediate post-war volumes, *Epitaphs and Occasions* (1949) and *Counterparts* (1954), that he was looking for his identity as a poet — something that he may be said to have found only with *Brutus's Orchard* in 1957.

   In the next decade one might argue that Fuller did "catch on" as a poet. For the poets of the Movement and the contributors to Ian Hamilton's seminal periodical, *The Review*, in the sixties, Fuller seemed an exemplar not only of the level-headed qualities that those writers wanted to see in English poetry, but also of the continuities with the poetry of the thirties that they felt to be strengthening and that they saw as having been broken by the New Romanticism of the forties.

   The sixties for Fuller were to culminate in a very prolific period poetically, with *New Poems* in 1968, *Tiny Tears* in 1973, and *From the Joke Shop* in 1975. He had experimented with syllabics in *New Poems*; and *From the Joke Shop* gives us a sequence of poems written in three-line sections of iambics or their syllabic equivalent, in which Fuller writes with great naturalness and fluency. Here we encounter what was, for the time, the authentic Fuller voice — urbane, tentative, exploratory, ironic. Looking over the titles of this impressive output of poems, one sees that there are an abundance of poems on scientific subjects ("The Approach of the Comet", "The Life of the Bee") and on art and the relation of art to reality ("Shakespeare and Co.", "Consolations of Art"). "Reading *The Bostonians* in Algeciras Bay" (from *New Poems* (1968)) may seem a long way from "To M.S., killed in Spain" (from *Poems* (1939)) — and it is, despite Fuller's nostalgic and ironic recollections of earlier days in the later poem. Yet there are important and clear continuities, not least of which is the Fuller voice — an attainment of rhythm and diction — that is the main mode of projection of the Fullerian attitudes throughout his work; and increasingly so, as that work matures. The interest in science and the concern with the relation of art to reality are really two aspects of the same preoccupation — the validity of the whole enterprise of poetry as a mode of relating to reality. This scepticism concerning art is not incongruous in one who began in an ethos where art was seen as having its justification in relation to action. The old Marxist apologia had long been abandoned; but a rational, questioning attitude to the function of art remained — and remained as a salutary concern.

It would be wrong to step easily from these observations to a sense that Fuller's scepticism concerning art derived from the life he had led, on the one hand, as a successful company solicitor, and, on the other, as a steady writer of poetry and fiction. In this respect, Fuller's career had a parallel in that of Wallace Stevens, whom Fuller came to admire; though Stevens, at the end of his career, refused the invitation to occupy the Charles Eliot Norton Chair at Harvard, because it might precipitate his retirement, whereas Fuller easily took on his appointment as Professor of Poetry at Oxford. Stevens's central preoccupation was with the role of art in a sceptical age; and in this his work must have been congenial to Fuller.

Perhaps, because Fuller's life does not give the impression of compartmentalisation that Stevens's life gave, he has seemed a less paradoxical figure. Yet there are paradoxical elements in his life, not the least of which is the intense drive to write manifested by this seemingly bourgeois, establishment figure. Fuller expressed great satisfaction with his public role as Governor of the B.B.C. He seems the equally happy exemplar of public and family virtues; and one is left asking, "Where is the Fuller *daemon*?" He writes with sensitivity and compassion about animals, with whom he seems to make an easy identification; yet, while his poems about Africa responded to the sense that "This awful ceremony of the doomed, unknown/And innocent victim has its replica/Embedded in our memories" ("The Plains"), he himself, as evidenced in the forms of his art, seemed unchanged at the deepest level. He always looks out with the conscientious British decency that has been a mark of his sensibility from the beginning. There is no Conradian sense of foundations being shaken. Indeed, while "The Plains" and other poems about the wildlife of Africa are powerful, his poems about African people, such as "Teba" or "The Tribes", are not among his most successful. He is most at home with the caged monkeys in "The Petty Officers' Mess", where the animals seem to mirror what is pathetically and domestically human, as do pets.

Nonetheless, one has the sense that, beneath the tightly contained Fuller decency and composure, there lurked doubts concerning the whole enterprise of civilisation and a feeling that the house might one day fall down on us — something that emerges to near explicitness in "What is Terrible" or "Night", also from Africa. That sense of things finally found a place in his domestic ambience in *Subsequent to Summer* (1985) and *Available for Dreams* (1989), through his awareness that his own life, along with the lives of those he has known and loved, was coming to a close. Within his garden he encounters constant evidence of the fragility of life and of the continuity of his own life with that of the animals he sees there; while, in his contemplations, the ironic oddness of the way things fall together is set over against the memory of how things once were. All this is reflected in discontinuities of form quite new to his poetry, but wholly in keeping with his vision.

It would be fanciful to find these paradoxes mirrored in the Fuller photographs, concerning which there are so many jokes. No doubt the image of a "retired major-general" that seems often to come through has a lot to do with the set facial poses sought by professional photographers; though it has to be admitted that, even in the shot in his old Daimler for the *Crime Omnibus*, he looks very much the part. In less formal photographs, the facial expression reveals the self-effacing, tender aspects of character that are part of one's experience of him as a person and a poet.

For all his sense that he was a poet who did not catch on, Fuller's poetry is importantly central to the development of British poetry in this century. His first book, *Poems* from 1939, shows two important influences, that of Auden and that of Graves (mediated in part through the poetry of Norman Cameron). Auden, and Graves (despite his later protestations), adapted the revolution of Anglo-American modernism to the traditions of British poetry. Auden's poetry, with its industrial imagery, its tensions between the liberal ideals of the personal life and the radical demands of public commitment in the thirties, its accommodation of contemporary speech and traditional forms, was the basis for the poetry of Fuller and his friends from *Twentieth Century Verse*, and remained for Fuller a continuing influence. Coming to maturity after the rise of Hitler, Fuller took politics as a natural and abiding ambience in the way that it was not for Auden and his upper-middle class contemporaries, who grew up in the twenties. Fuller's radicalism was deepened by his experiences in World War II, and it remained an essential part of his reaction to events, never to be abandoned entirely.

These tendencies were carried by Fuller through the New Romanticism of the forties and the doldrums of the difficult period of cultural adaptation after World War II, to become a part of his mature idiom in the days of his great poetic flowering in the seventies. In between lay *Collected Poems* (1962) — "a bit premature" as he once put it — a book that encapsulated the traditions that he had kept alive and that helped to make him the older poet to whom those associated with *New Lines* and with Ian Hamilton's *The Review* in the sixties could look up as an upholder of the poetic values that they stood for. These traditions of poetic form and of attitude are carried forward to the full display of their power — if that is the word for an achievement so unself-assertive — in *Subsequent to Summer* and *Available for Dreams*.

An equally important continuity to be found in Fuller's poetry is a cultural one. Despite his own sense that he never caught on, his poetry has a perhaps unequalled significance as a record of what it was to be British through the many changes that Fuller experienced: the depression; the war; the gradual sense of the declining centrality of British culture in the years following the war; and that deep sense of the richness and importance of domestic life that emerges in his later work. It would be hard to point to any poet who has more to offer in this respect.

However one may wish to view it or explain it, Roy Fuller's *oeuvre* is impressive and substantial. It contains an undoubted masterpiece, *Available for Dreams* — one of the outstanding collections of poetry in English from this half of the century. His other collections have sustained a very high standard; and their very consistency may have resulted in his being taken for granted. His Oxford Lectures, while not meeting the demand that they be "exciting" or "innovative" — so much the expectation concerning criticism today — are powerfully perceptive and can be returned to regularly with profit and delight. Indeed, there is pleasure in almost everything he has written. And, if we set his career beside that of poets who "caught on" — Auden, MacNeice, Dylan Thomas, even Philip Larkin — we see no falling off or drying up, but a poetic achievement of remarkable consistency — and one that got better and better.

This very remarkable achievement of Roy Fuller, as well as the experience of his friendship, is what the contributors to this volume had come together to celebrate and explore in anticipation of his eightieth birthday. They had done so with the feeling that, in the case of work of a high order, there can be no finer compliment than a candid exploration of what it has to offer; and it is in this spirit that the criticisms in this book were written. While the book was with the publisher, news came of Roy Fuller's death. It was felt that the book, as originally conceived and written, offered an appropriate tribute to his memory.

A.T. Tolley

JOHN FULLER

The Garden
For my father

Considering that the world needs to be born
Endlessly out of our looking at it, it's no wonder that
We retire here for that purpose in our brief time.

Mappers and model-makers, traffickers
In language's unreliable schedules, all our
Journeying is a nostalgia for this.

The garden bears our traces and becomes
Through them the model of a mind which thus
Defines itself: a part, and yet apart.

The world may grow here. All that is left outside
Is unimaginable, all within
So like itself that there is nothing else.

Blossom is rumoured. The mind also prepares
Its own best growth, pruning just beyond
The bud. Though summer is already past.

Leaves that would fly have lately fallen. Lifted
Once in wind, they have now become detached,
Ready to drift. And autumn, too, is gone.

Those purer spirits whose undeliberate music
Also creates a more or less habitual space
Have turned their retreat into a coded return.

These pebbled paths lead only to a point
Which shows where they have come from and that now
To continue is a figure not a journey.

Those walls were built no higher than they need be
And where they join give reasons for joining. Where not,
Is a hinge never still enough to cease to be one.

For to enter is always possible, as it is
To leave, though to do neither is at last
As much a relief as both were ridiculous.

If others care to overlook these long
Endeavours, let them, for after all we are
Contented merely with corroboration.

Should there be some claim to distinction (or
That price of distinction, the distance between truth
And friendliness) then truth will decide the matter.

The solemnest face caught staring in would be
Your own. The reason that it never is
Seems like the reason for almost everything.

We are, possibly, posed this riddle early
In life: which is the likeliest of mirrors,
The face that reflects the world, or another face?

The last is not easily admitted, the first
The one we know. It is a grief that placed
Together they only do what mirrors do.

Reflections of reflections, it is said,
Are a symbol of all desire. And lead nowhere
But endlessly and shallow into themselves.

To see oneself in the garden is the final
Privilege, the last illusion like
The glittering letters in a burning leaf.

To be an image of the thing already
Containing you is surely a fine prospect,
As the fruit is an eager portrait of the tree.

And being so requires the greatest detachment,
Function of the philosopher's particular passion
To locate beauty beyond its short-lived shapes.

The garden, therefore, is a signal comfort
To those who fear that belonging is an illusion
Like longing itself, like the desire for desire.

For though it takes no pleasure in itself,
The garden is beautiful while you are in it,
And having once been you are always there.

GAVIN EWART

The Counting Out
(i.m. Roy Fuller, d. September 27th 1991)

Writers old and writers new
have a time and have a cue,
every girl and every boy
ends like Sylvia, Tom or Roy.

Counting out is in the song,
can be short or can be long.
They dance round but they all know
in the end they have to go.

Young ones happy in the sun
have their fling and have their fun
turning in the three times three —
till they stop — and out goes *he*!

Raise a tune and raise a shout,
we are in the counting out;
eyes and ears and stiffened joints,
we go when the finger points!

BERNARD BERGONZI

The Poet in Wartime

Roy Fuller published two collections of poetry during the war, both
with thematically resonant titles, *The Middle of a War* (1942) and
The Lost Season (1944). The former contains "January 1940", a brief
satirical history of English poetry, which concludes with the lines:

> Donne, alive in his shroud,
> Shakespeare, in the coil of a cloud,
> Saw death very well as he
> Came crab-wise, dark and massy.
> I envy not only their talents
> And fertile lack of balance
> But the appearance of choice
> In their sad and fatal voice.

As the original title indicates, the poem was written during the
strange period of the Phoney War, which lasted from September 1939
to April 1940, when Hitler occupied Denmark and Norway and went
on to invade and conquer Holland, Belgium and France. In January
1940 all that lay in the future, as did the Battle of Britain and the
bombing of London. Roy Fuller himself was still a civilian, and the
encounter with death on which the poem dwells, though already a
possibility, was not yet an immediate one. When Fuller's *Collected
Poems* appeared in 1962 the title had been changed to "War Poet",
which gave the poem a rather different significance. Fuller had served
in the navy and survived the war, had written a distinguished body of
poetry in response to it, and had himself been placed in the category
of "war poet".

How far Fuller deserves this title is a matter of definition. It orig-
inated in the First World War, and it was applied first to Rupert
Brooke, who died of blood poisoning on the way to battle, and then
to the trench poets of the Western Front, like Siegfried Sassoon and
Wilfred Owen. During the 1939–45 war there were regular calls for
the appearance of war poets, but they were not so easy to identify.
The contrast between soldiers in danger at the Front and civilians living in ignoble safety at home, which provoked the trench poets, was
no longer so evident. In fact, civilians might be in greater danger from

the bombing of cities than servicemen in remote camps, and anxiety about families being bombed recurs in the poems and stories of Alun Lewis; the wife of the Apocalyptic poet J.F. Hendry was killed in an air raid. Nevertheless, some recognisable war poets did emerge among men in uniform. Keith Douglas, generally agreed to be the finest of them, admired, and identified with, the trench poets of the earlier war. He upheld a high and narrow ideal of the war poet, restricting it to those who like Sassoon and Owen and Rosenberg — and himself — had been in action, and contemptuously denying it to the staff-officers and base-wallahs who contributed to anthologies of soldiers' verse. Douglas, though, was an unusual, perhaps anachronistic figure, equally dedicated to the vocations of poet and soldier.

There were other poets, who might be best described as civilians in uniform, with families at home, for whom the war was a series of experiences of loss, deprivation, separation and boredom rather than of violent action. There was no equivalent for the British in the Second World War of the mechanized slaughter of the Western Front, and casualties were far lower. The only campaign where British troops were continually in action from 1940 to 1943 was in the North African desert, which produced the war poetry of Douglas, Hamish Henderson and John Jarmain. Other writers were in the services for several years but never saw action. This was true of Alun Lewis, who received posthumous fame as a war poet — though his death in 1944 was reportedly accidental but possibly suicide — and of Roy Fuller. In fact, some of Fuller's best poems about the war were written before he was called up into the navy in 1941. He describes in his memoirs, *The Strange and the Good*, how after war was declared on the morning of 3rd September 1939 he self-consciously lay down in a shallow trench he had dug in his back garden when an air-raid warning sounded, though it soon proved to be a false alarm. Later that day he went to visit his friend Julian Symons, and just over a year later, on 7th September 1940, Fuller sat with Symons in a suburban park watching the Luftwaffe begin the bombing of the capital: "neat formations of German bombers, with attendant frisky-puppy fighters, moving overhead to raid the London docks. Soon, slating cloud-mountains of smoke were seen rising from that area. This was more like *Things to Come*".[1] Fuller refers to Alexander Korda's famous film of a book by H.G. Wells, made in 1936, which provided potent images of the coming war and placed the bombing of London, accurately enough, in 1940.

Fuller's first book, *Poems*, had been published in December 1939, enabling him — just — to be regarded as a poet of the 1930s. The influence of Auden is evident in language and themes as well as in the fashionably laconic title. Peter Levi, in his Oxford lecture on Auden, refers to the inadequacy of that poet's response to the events of 1940, compared with that of certain French and German poets, and of Fuller, whom he refers to as "less mature as a poet and far less fluent than Auden, but genuine, real, our own."[2] Furthermore, Fuller, unlike Auden, was there on the historical spot when the Battle of Britain was fought and London was bombed. Levi's point is well taken and can, I think, be developed. Fuller was an Audenesque poet in more than style and diction; he shared Auden's capacity for significant generalization, for seeing civilization as a map where everything can be located and named, and for presenting historical forces as types and symbols. The tendency towards generalization and symbol remained throughout Fuller's long career as a poet, but in the context of 1940 it had particular urgency and point. War and the prospect of bombing had dominated the literary imagination for several years: in the Korda-Wells film, in novels by Graham Greene and George Orwell, in poems by Auden and MacNeice, and in many other instances. Then, in 1940, it happened; Auden's words about Spain, "our fever's menacing shapes are precise and alive", had a fresh application. Auden was not there to see it, but his admirer and disciple Fuller was, and in his poems of 1940–41 he is not only describing the physical impact of war, but enacting both the fulfilment and the dissolution of a major myth. In the late 1930s it was assumed that the looming war would be a terminal disaster. In showing life going on amid the ruins of London (also, in more than one sense, the ruins of the myth), Fuller, whilst remaining an Audenesque poet, is going beyond Auden. Or to put it differently, he is writing the poems that Auden might have written if he had stayed in England.

Fuller's "Epitaph on a Bombing Victim" is a simple and straightforward example of the process, invoking History, that inescapable presence in the poetry of the 1930s:

> Reader, could his limbs be found
> Here would lie a common man:
> History inflicts no wound
> But explodes what it began,
> And with its enormous lust
> For division splits the dust.
> Do not ask his nation; that
> Was History's confederate.

In other poems Fuller responds in more extended and complex ways to the crisis that has moved out of brooding imagination into destructive reality; in, for instance, "Summer 1940", "Soliloquy in an Air Raid", and "Autumn 1940", which begins:

> No longer can guns be cancelled by love,
> Or by rich paintings in the galleries;
> The music in the icy air cannot live,
> The autumn has blown away the rose.
>
> Can we be sorry that those explosions
> Which occurring in Spain and China reached us as
> The outer ring of yearning emotions,
> Are here as rubble and fear, as metal and glass,
>
> Are here in the streets, in the sewers full of people?
> We see as inevitable and with relief
> The smoke from shells like plump ghosts on the purple,
> The bombers, black insect eggs, on the sky's broad leaf.

The poem ends with a sober expression of the Marxist hope to which Fuller still clung, with an echo of Auden's "Spain":

> today the caught-up-breath —
> The exhalation is promised for tomorrow.
>
> And changed tomorrow is promised precisely by
> The measure of the engendered hate, the hurt
> Descended; the instinct and capacity
> Of man for happiness, and that drowned art.

Perhaps the finest poem of this phase of Fuller's work is "To My Wife", which opens with a superb display of Audenesque eloquence and rhetoric but moves on to a directness and vulnerability of feeling uncommon in Auden:

> The loud mechanical voices of the sirens
> Lure me from sleep and on the heath, like stars,
> Moths fall into a mounting shaft of light.
> Aircraft whirr over and then the night stays quiet;
> The moon is peeled of clouds, its gold is changed
> On stone for silver and the cap of sky
> Glitters like quartz, impersonal and remote.
> The surface is the same: the clock's bland face,
> Its smiling moustaches, hide the spring, knotted
> Like muscles, and the crouching jungle hammer.

The same but so different with you not here.
This evening when I turned from the clothes you left,
Empty and silk, the souls of swallows flickered
Against the glass of our house: I felt no better
Along the tree-massed alleys where I saw
The long pale legs on benches in the dark.
It was no vague nostalgia which I breathed
Between the purple colloids of the air:
My lust was as precise and fierce as that of
The wedge-headed jaguar or the travelling Flaubert. . .

Fuller's wife and young son (later the poet John Fuller) were at that time evacuated to her family in the north of England. The sense of separation was to become pervasive in the poems that Fuller wrote after he joined the navy, and which have earned him the title of "war poet", though he was perhaps in greater danger in the blitz than in the armed forces. Although he was a qualified solicitor he was made a radar mechanic in the Fleet Air Arm, serving first in England, then in East Africa; in the last phase of the war he was back in London with a commission and a desk job at the Admiralty. The poems that Fuller wrote between 1941 and 1945, particularly those collected in *The Middle of a War*, are neat, astringent and depressed, expressing the boredom and sense of loss that recur throughout the prose and poetry of the Second World War, and which was so much less dramatic than the satirical anger of Sassoon or the fierce pity of Owen. The titles tell their own story: "ABC of a Naval Trainee", "Defending the Harbour", "Royal Naval Air Station", "Saturday Night in a Sailors' Home", "The End of a Leave", "The Middle of a War", "Waiting to be Drafted", "Y.M.C.A. Writing Room", "Good-Bye for a Long Time", "Troopship". "Royal Naval Air Station" is one of the best and most representative of the prevailing sensibility of civilians in uniform. It is also characteristic of Fuller in its movement from precise observation to generalization and typification:

> The piano, hollow and sentimental, plays,
> And outside, falling in a moonlit haze,
> The rain is endless as the empty days.
>
> Here in the mess, on beds, on benches, fall
> The blue serge limbs in shapes fantastical:
> The photographs of girls are on the wall.
>
> And the songs of the minute walk into our ears;
> Behind the easy words are difficult tears:
> The pain which stabs is dragged out over years.

A ghost has made uneasy every bed.
You are not you without me and *The dead*
Only are pleased to be alone it said.

And hearing it silently the living cry
To be again themselves, or sleeping try
To dream it is impossible to die.

The mood and the endless rain recall one of the most famous poems
of the war, Alun Lewis's "All Day It Has Rained". But Fuller, here
and in similar poems, seems less a mere victim of circumstance than
Lewis. The response, though despondent, is tougher; the poet feels
part of a community enduring boredom and separation from loved
ones and meaningful existence, and attempts to grasp and place the
experience in general and not merely personal terms.

Fuller's period in East Africa did not greatly change the tone of
his poetry, but it brought fresh subject matter. In "The White Conscript and the Black Conscript", for instance, he struggles to make
sense, in loosely Marxist terms, of the gulf separating black and white
soldiers. Two of the best poems in *A Lost Season* are "Giraffes" and
"The Plains", where Fuller looks at African flora and fauna with his
characteristic juxtaposition of exact observation and ready general
statement; they may show the influence of Rilke, whom so many poets during the war read, admired and imitated. After returning to
England Fuller found himself once more under enemy bombardment,
as he had been in the blitz of 1940–41; this time from the German
V1 flying bombs in the summer of 1944 and then from V2 rockets
in the winter of 1944–45. His poem "During a Bombardment by V-
Weapons" catches the strange feeling of the last winter of the war
in London, when the end was in sight but sudden death from a V2
rocket could still descend without warning at any moment (the bombardment continued until March 1945, within a few weeks of the end
of the war; it gets into literature in *Ninety Eighty-Four* and *Gravity's
Rainbow*):

The little noises of the house:
Drippings between the slates and ceiling;
From the electric fire's cooling,
Tickings; the dry feet of a mouse:

These at the ending of a war
Have power to alarm me more
Than the ridiculous detonations
Outside the gently coughing curtains.

And, love, I see your pallor bears
A far more pointed threat than steel.
Now all the permanent and real
Furies are settling in upstairs.

The small threats of the coming peace are somehow more "real" than the large-scale terrors of war. In the phrase "the gently coughing curtains" Fuller offers a wonderfully precise rendering of something which I clearly recall from that time: the slight stirring of curtains at a distant explosion.

In 1965 Fuller wrote, "I think war service exorcized several evils that might have gone on constricting me as a poet. In Caudwell's term, it exchanged reality for illusion, and after the war, following an awkward period of adjustment, I was able to write verse of rather wider scope."[3] Subsequently, in *The Strange and the Good*, Fuller expressed dissatisfaction with his war poems and what he saw as their limited range: "The poems' dominating theme was separation; a characteristic. . .of far too much of the verse of the Second World War, particularly in domestic and backward-looking circumstances (though this objection, which even a guilty party like myself held strongly, had to be modified when, after the war, Keith Douglas's collected poems appeared, and later still when Alun Ross collected his revised war poems in *Open Sea*)".[4] Fuller appears to be unfavourably comparing his kind of poetry, with its personal and domestic themes, with that of the poets who had seen action, such as Douglas and Alan Ross. His reference to Ross is significant, for he was a naval poet who had been in battle, and whose poems, published well after the war, reflected his experience. This is particularly true of his major work, "JW51B", a poem of some 500 lines about the Battle of the Barents Sea, a naval action fought in near-darkness in Arctic waters off the coast of North Russia in December 1942. Ross draws on his own experience; the destroyer he was serving on was shelled and crippled by a larger German warship, he had several comrades killed around him and was himself in mortal danger fighting fires. He describes all this superbly in his autobiography, *Blindfold Games*, but in the poem he does not mention himself, aiming at epical, impersonal treatment of the battle.

Ross was a war poet in Douglas's strict sense, but this did not stop him from greatly admiring Fuller, as he recalls in *Blindfold Games*: "I came to know nearly all Roy Fuller's poems by heart and it would have surprised me then, reading admiringly on my bunk in *Badger* before whisky took its toll or the padre hauled me out for a nightcap, if I had known he was to become one of my closest friends. The poems of separation from his wife and son which he wrote then came to touch me as if I had known them in real life as well as on the page".[5] Ross, the poet who had been in violent action, here implicitly refutes Fuller's self-criticism for writing only of separation and loss: it is a satisfying juxtaposition of the two most distinguished poets of the Second World War to serve in the navy, and whose experiences are complementary. Separation and danger are both preoccupations of the poet in wartime.

NOTES

1. Roy Fuller, *The Strange and the Good: Collected Memoirs* (London: Collins Harvill, 1989) 199–200.
2. Peter Levi, *The Art of Poetry* (London and New Haven: Yale University Press, 1991) 239.
3. In Ian Hamilton (ed.), *The Poetry of War 1939–1945* (1965); paperback edition (London: New English Library, 1972) 164.
4. *The Strange and the Good*, 239.
5. Alan Ross, *Blindfold Games* (London: Collins Harvill, 1988) 240.

Donald E. Stanford

The Poetry of Roy Fuller, 1959 – 1980

I first became acquainted with the poetry of Roy Fuller in December 1971 when, in the office of *The Southern Review*, as I was glancing at a review copy of his Oxford lectures on poetry, *Owls and Artificers*, I came across his perceptive remarks on the syllabic verse of Elizabeth Daryush, the daughter of Robert Bridges. I had long considered Daryush an important contemporary poet, but she was not well known in America, and I had believed that she was also being down-graded or ignored in England. But here was the Oxford Professor of Poetry writing an informed critique of an important aspect of her work. I finished the book and then looked up Fuller's own poetry in the library (he was not at that time well-known in America), and then lost no time in inviting him to contribute to the *Review* and in arranging a meeting with him in London the coming summer.

What impressed me when I read Fuller's poetry for the first time was his competence in the use of metrical language (as distinct from free verse) and the variety of his traditional verse forms. He was practising what he preached when he quoted his friend Allen Tate in an Oxford lecture: "Formal versification is the primary structure of poetic order, the assurance to the reader and to the poet himself that the poet is in control of the disorder outside himself and within his own mind."[1] The poetic scene in America in 1971 was discouraging to an editor who favoured formalist poetry. It was cluttered with the remnants of Ezra Pound's Imagist revolution that had occurred sixty years previously - structureless so-called free verse (much of it confessional), non-rhythmical prose broken up into short lines to masquerade as poetry. But in Fuller's work, the formalist tradition was obviously thriving. I hoped his success might encourage a revival of formalism among our younger poets.

Fuller was committing what was then considered in America a capital offence — the writing and publishing of sonnet sequences. In fact, some of his most challenging poetry is written in this genre.

"Mythological Sonnets" in Fuller's 1957 volume *Brutus's Orchard* is a meditation in nineteen poems on the power of sex from ancient times when

> Their girls were ground under the enormous thews
> Of visiting gods, watched by staid munching ewes

to contemporary London where

> Even the most serene and opulent
> Goddesses rise from the sordid life of man,
> Who catching, say, a girl in stockinged feet
> Arranging a shop-window sees the event
> Translated to a new and staggering span
> Of art, the previous pantheon obsolete.

The power of sex resides principally in the eternal female whose ascendancy over the male lapses only temporarily during the sexual act:

> Nothing can still that agonizing rage
> For what was never ruled but for an hour
> And now lies far beyond the sceptre's power.

There is a continuous juxtaposition between the classical world of Homer and Ovid and the twentieth century — during which various manifestation of passion, jealousy, and lust (sometimes frustrated) are presented, including the attempted rape of Deianira by "Cheiron, the centaur":

> When the sad, baffled beast with clumsy hooves,
> Paws impotently at the delicate
> And now relenting limbs.

The mythological scenes are written in a style tense and graphic illustrating the belief of the poet who claims

> we will feel
> Compared with myths contemporary life unreal.

Those critics who have faulted Fuller's poetry as tame and passionless may wish to have another look at "Mythological Sonnets".

The writing of a series of twenty-one sonnets in the sixteen line, a b b a, stanza form of Meredith's "Modern Love" (just one hundred years after that work's first publication) is, from a technical point of view, a considerable accomplishment.

An implicit theme of the poem is the poet caught between his creative, imaginary life and what an American poet, Wallace Stevens, in a similar situation called "the malady of the quotidian" ("The Man

Whose Pharynx Was Bad"), which includes the numbing nature of the business world and the trivialities of city life.

The protagonist of "Meredithian Sonnets" is not Fuller, he is not even a poet though perhaps a poet manqué, but he sometimes looks on the world of nature with an artist's and a poet's eyes:

> The autumn wind had sounded through the night,
> But stepping in the garden after dawn
> He sees the flowers round the wounded lawn
> Like posters, all their valleys filled with light.
>
>   . . .
>
> On chocolate furrows birds like snowballs stand
> While horses scissor pieces of the skies....
> And larks rise through disintegrating smoke
> And see it is an island that they sing.

He feels that his imagination and sensitivity have become blighted in the daily vulgarities he encounters in the city.

> Our cheap, scarred times have bred the usurious mind
> And substituted fresco for mosaic.

The major, explicit theme of the poem may be appropriately designated by Meredith's title, "Modern Love." This modern lover, a post-war Prufrock, is tortured with desires he is unable to satisfy, unhappily married, unsuccessful in an attempted affair with the maid servant in the attic, suffering from sexual fantasies

> Stopping at photographs of girls with flowers
> For nipples and with thighs beyond his powers.

He attempts to find refuge in fleeting dreams of Asiatic love and lust, and finally resigns himself to dreary reality, more betrayed (to alter Meredith's words) by what is false without than by what is false within.

The protagonist of the sonnet sequence "The Historian" is not a poet but an aging historian, yet he is in some ways a self-analytical spokesman for Fuller. The first line of the first sonnet, "The scene my study: Faustian locale", links "The Historian" with several other poems by Fuller on the Faustian theme. The historian, speaking in the first person, states that he is suffering from a minor ill. In a recent excursion to the Tower of London, as he mingled with the infected crowd on the bridge, he caught the bug of — history! Even historians, it seems, are not immune to it. One result of being bitten by this bug is an obsessive tendency to examine the present in terms of the past and of the imagined future with reference to the British empire, the remnants of which he is now experiencing (which naturally draws in comparisons with other empires). At the same time there is a self-conscious examination of the historian protagonist himself—his successes, weaknesses, failures, disillusionments. Thus viewed, "The Historian" is closely related to much of Fuller's poetry, which consists of a scrupulous examination of himself and of the society in which he lives. The net result of these private and public speculations is not exhilarating. He believes that the young (that is the future) will regard his accomplishments with indifference:

> Youth that brings down or hoists the crown looks past
> My work and face with equal indifference.

As to the future of the state and of society:

> my hope is only
> That blood will not be spilt and that each side
> Will with defeat be somehow satisfied.

We should note that this poem was written and published in the 1960s when the cold war was at its height and there was a real danger that "each side", that is the Russian bloc and the NATO bloc, would destroy each other in a nuclear war.

The prevailing mood of the series is one of ironical, stoic resignation, but there is plenty of opportunity, as the historian examines the follies of the past and present, for Fuller to employ his brilliant verbal wit, which ranges from the tender to the caustic.

"To X", a series of twenty-one thirteen-line stanzas arranged in the form of roundels, the repeated rhymes and phrases of which require great inventiveness on the part of the poet, bears resemblances in structure and subject matter to the three sonnet series just discussed. Like the "Meredithian Sonnets", it tells a tale of modern love, written in the first person, by the protagonist, a Prufrockian bachelor who suffers the agonies of a love affair with a married younger woman at a beach resort. The affair is never consummated, but so low has this anti-hero sunk in his own regard, he can take a bleak satisfaction in the fact that he can still feel pain at least, if not sexual pleasure:

> Your beauty promised scorn, your youth disdain:
> Perhaps I let you think of me as cold.
> To find oneself still capable of pain
> Was direly reassuring, being old.

At first glance "To X" appears to be a clever tour de force, but in retrospect the suffering of this anti-hero takes on an unexpectedly haunting depth, perhaps because it is expressed in such an intricately resonant form:

> Shaken by longing, how can one conceive
> That longing is the essence of it all?

In the three decades 1950–1980 Fuller published close to three hundred poems. Of these, I would like to discuss a few that I consider among the important (in addition to those already discussed) or that hold for me a special attraction.

Fuller himself has reminded us that the "I" of a poem is not necessarily the author. On the other hand, as we have seen, the persona may be at least partially the author and may be mediating certain ideas and experiences of the author. A case in point is "The Ides of March". The first person narrator is Brutus — an historical, Shakesperian, and imaginary composite. The poem presents a graphic, convincing external and psychological portrait of Brutus in his orchard hesitating, wavering in his decision to join the terrorists conspiring against the State — that is, against Caesar. It is probable that this psychological delineation of Brutus is informed by Fuller's own political withdrawal from a belief in active Marxism to acceptance of bourgeois capitalism and democracy — though of course Fuller moved in a direction opposite to that of Brutus. Fuller was a family man (one of his best poems is entitled "Family Matters") and Brutus has his wife much on his mind as he meditates his final decision:

> I hope my wife will walk out of the house
> While I am in their compromising presence,
> And know that what we built had no foundation
> Other than luck and my false privileged role
> In a society that I despised.

So Fuller may once have despised the society in which he lived — but long before he wrote this poem. "The Ides of March" is in beautifully written blank verse. I suspect it may have been one of the poet's favourite poems.

Another political poem of note is "Florestan to Leonora" which has, with the sudden and surprising liberation of eastern European countries in 1989, even more relevance today than it had on its first publication in the 1950s. Shortly after their first heady enthusiasm for their newly won freedom, some from the liberated countries were not sure that freedom was better than the economic security of communist repression. The poem, Fuller has told us, "was prompted by seeing a production of Beethoven's *Fidelio* by the Stuttgart Opera Company." In the opera Florestan's wife, Leonora, disguised as Fidelio, succeeds in saving her imprisoned husband's life and bringing him to freedom. The assumption is that both husband and wife are equally happy in Florestan's escape. Fuller, however, casts doubt on that assumption. Florestan faces the prospect of freedom with reluctance and trepidation, especially as it was won for him by his wife. He had, in fact, become used to confinement because he had been able to maintain his own values there. Now, he tells his wife:

> Our values must shrivel to the size of those
> Held by a class content with happiness . . .

The poem appears to be a pejorative evaluation of British society in the 1950s and the reference to Florestan's insomnia at the end of the poem further suggests its autobiographical nature, for Fuller referred to his own insomnia in several other poems.

Another poem with political implications, "Translation", has been widely well-received. The protagonist is Cinna in Shakespeare's *Julius Caesar* who "has ceased to matter", as well as a stand-in for Fuller:

> From progressive organisations, from quarterlies
> Devoted to daring verse, from membership of
> Committees, from letters of various protest
>   I shall withdraw forthwith.

The poem marks the end of Fuller's belief in the value of political activism.

What has frequently given me the most pleasure in Fuller's poetry is his varied and highly original responses to the world of nature, beginning early in his career with the elegant descriptions of the animals of Africa and continuing down to the present with his accounts of the curious behaviour of flora and fauna in his home and garden. In poem after poem we see this garden in all seasons of the year and in all weathers. I have the impression that he did not go in for long exhausting nature excursions. He found all he needed at his home, 37 Langton Way, and the adjacent fields of Blackheath.

Tendrils, for example. Who but Fuller could or would write an interesting poem ("Creeper") on a vine that has dared to enter his house:

Probing filament, what do you seek
In our affairs? You have waited too
Long to arrive, in any event,
For your pallid reach must fail soon, not
Even leave a dry whisker, perhaps.

He had a proclivity for spiders and was unhappy when he discovered
"a spider drowned, like a scribble, in a bucket." In "The Image", a
spider, "A half loved creature, motionless and bloated", is removed
unhurt from the bathtub and deposited in the garden. Larkin selected
this poem for his anthology of twentieth-century poetry. A somewhat
different perception of spiders occurs in one of his cinquains (modelled
on those of Adelaide Crapsey):

Spiders,
With all their legs,
Over irregular
Terrain step lightly as well-bred
Horses.

Birds have been present in English poetry for centuries, but they have
never been observed with a sharper or more unusual eye than Fuller's.
Of a pigeon:

All who will closely look at one espy
A geometrical and insane eye.

Of a starling he notes

one extended bored
Tea-sipper's claw.

and of a budgerigar's eye he remarks that the

bead of jet is closed
By an incredibly neat suture.

He notes again that

the pigeon's eye blinks as slowly as
An old-fashioned camera's shutter.

"In His Sixty-Fifth Year" opens with a stanza on a starling:

With beak about as long and hinged as chopsticks,
The starling stabbing among the chocolate whorls
Is speckled like a specimen of quartz,

Except the slanted settings for the eyes
Which are as dark as those of belly-dancers.

In his long poem "The Historian" there is a passing reference to birds
in winter:

To see bare branches, and the ghostly tits
Ever appear and reappear without
Overt existence in between.

Anyone who has watched titmice (as these birds are usually called
in America) on a feeder or in the woods as they move from perch to
perch with lightning speed will appreciate the magical accuracy of the
phrases "without/ Overt existence in between." These are only a few
of the incidental felicities among Fuller's many references to birds.

He is equally adept at presenting bees, blossoms, flowers, small
animals and countless other forms of organic life. I like especially the
opening stanza of "Apple Tree" —

I puzzle why the flowering tree
Is also in song, until I see
Each flower's stigma is a bee.

His nature poems are sometimes purely descriptive, but frequently
his observations lead to ethical considerations, as in "The Life of the
Bee." In pursuing "the duty of their race" the

bees accept a common life
Yet do their fellow bees the smallest harm
That's possible.

And at times nature observations lead to metaphysical speculation as
in "The Lawn, Spring and Summer" where he congratulates a tree-
rat upon encountering a "green and reasonably buried walnut" and
advises him:

Live with your death, your species' death — with craft,
That on this globe, and those unknown and past,
The gases and the carbon spirals clasp
A spirit fearful but immortal somewhere.

Fuller rejected a major principle of Pound's free-verse, imagist revolution when he chose to write his poems in metrical language and
traditional verse forms, but he accepted another principle of the movement whole-heartedly — that no subject should be closed to the modern poet. More than any other contemporary poet, Fuller, has, while

writing much of his poetry on the major central themes of human experience, also undertaken to explore the tiniest cracks and crevices of daily living in an attempt to discover material for a poem.

Who but Fuller would compose poems like "Metamorphoses" — about the reassurance he felt when, while disgustedly watching the mother of a new born baby buying junk food at a neighbourhood bakery, he suddenly realised that the food would soon be transformed into wholesome milk. The poem made Larkin's anthology of twentieth-century poetry. Then there is "Kitchen Life", written in the "imbecile medium" of free verse because it is appropriate for the subject. The poem describes the attempt to transfix a pea rolling uncontrolled in the kitchen sink. Among other poems successfully presenting subjects unlikely to be treated in verse are "The Autobiography of a Lung-worm", "Song in a Wood" in which an abandoned condom sings of the lovers who had used it — the "happy murderers" of future generations, and a poem on window-cleaners and another on the purchase for kitchen use of a spatter guard.

The poems as a whole are a comprehensive, perceptive record of the life of the poet as he commutes daily on the 53 bus from his home to his office, although his office life is generally left to his novels. The poems give accounts of his family relationships, love of music, recondite reading during nights of insomnia, dining, drinking, and friendships, changing political views, and observations on almost anything that grows or moves in his garden. A few of his poems on political matters are ironic and cold, but generally there is a very wide range of feeling projected in those poems dealing with human beings and with his own mental and emotional life. He never resorts to violent sensationalism. The dominant tone, especially in the later poems, is that of his own voice expressing the love and affection of a sensitive, humane and civilized man.

NOTE

1. Quoted in *Owls and Artificers* (London: Deutsch, 1971) 64.

Jonathan Barker

"The Amazing Pleasures of the Human": The Later Poems of Roy Fuller

Roy Fuller produced two volumes of collected poems; *Collected Poems 1936–61* in 1962, and the more recent *New and Collected Poems 1934–84* in 1985. Following publication of each, his work took new directions. After *Collected Poems 1936–61* we had first *Buff* and then the unrhymed syllabics of the remarkable *New Poems* of 1968, where a new tone transcended the last vestiges of the one-time influences of Auden and Yeats. Here begins the mature Fuller style of writing, which appears artlessly direct and plain but actually exhibits a wide range of technical experimentation. Throughout his writing life Fuller was consistently one of the most technically inventive of contemporary poets, continually ready to invent a new form or, through experiment, give new life to one existing already. *New Poems*, for instance, contains experiments with syllabic metres along the lines of the verse of Marianne Moore and Elizabeth Daryush (daughter of Robert Bridges), both of whose work he championed. This essay will look at the new directions taken following publication of his *New and Collected Poems 1934 – 84*.

Like Geoffrey Grigson, Fuller, in my view, produced some of his most original writing in the latter part of his career. In Fuller's case this late flowering was connected to a lifelong rejection of romantic rhetoric in favour of a precise expression of objective truthfulness to a specific everyday reality. In this he was a precursor of the Movement poets, a literary-historical fact even today not widely enough acknowledged. The inimitable Fuller tone consists of a wry directness which is coolly objective rather than impassioned, simultaneously human and heartfelt, and never cold. It is a poetry equally far removed from the rhetorical flourish of the forties or from a Gravesian sense of poetry as essentially rejecting contemporary reality in favour of expressing so-called "timeless" themes.

Although his first book was not published until 1939, we should remember that Fuller, along with his near contemporaries Geoffrey Grigson and Julian Symons, was at heart essentially a man of the thirties. His work always expressed a wide range of personal and cultural things, taking in equally individual, socio-political and intellectual topics. He has written poems on a very wide range of themes —

from scientific ideas to a spider in the bath — as if to prove that all subjects may be accommodated in a poem. Today Edith Sitwell's inability to accept Fuller's poem "The Image" beginning, "A spider in the bath. The image noted", to my generation woefully betrays her limited views of poetry. In comparison the "I" of Fuller's poems is consistently modest and truthful, reflecting the whole life of an individual in a specific time and place.

Fuller's view of art is well summed up in a quotation from W.H. Auden's essay "Writing" (from *The Dyer's Hand*, 1963) in which Auden argues that poetry should disenchant us from untruths:

> Poetry is not magic. In so far as poetry, or any other of the arts, can be said to have an ulterior purpose, it is, by telling the truth, to disenchant and disintoxicate.[1]

This view of poetry's intellectual role underpins much of Fuller's poetry as in, say, the marvellous "At a Warwickshire Mansion" (first collected in *Brutus's Orchard*, 1957) which deals with the "magic and mystery" craved by the schizophrenic and the poet's more precise role of expressing the truth of a given world. Thus "telling the truth" disenchants us from what Auden memorably called "The romantic lie in the brain/Of the sensual man-in-the-street" and defines poetry as a rational, intellectual force. This in turn leads to one other important aspect of Fuller's work — the sheer readability of the poems. This stems directly from a professional and craftsmanlike pride in making the poem as intelligible as possible, and a sense that, in a complex world, the poet should respect the reader and be as lucid as possible, the better to disenchant and disintoxicate us from untruths.

Fuller wrote sequences throughout his career, from the wartime "Winter in Camp", the "Meredithian Sonnets", "The Historian", to the book length *From the Joke Shop* of 1975. However, many of his very best sequences belong to his later work. An example is the "Mianserin Sonnets" sequence of twenty-one poems, which takes its name from a prescribed drug with the side-effect of creating vivid dreams, and which closes *New and Collected Poems 1934 – 84*. The first lines of "The Ants", the opening poem in the sequence, provides a good starting point for a look at some of the qualities of later Fuller:

> Ants at a bus-stop in the Old Kent Road;
> Four waltzing round the pavement at my feet;
> Typically aimless, late to be abroad
> (Clear in the sodium-illumined street),
> It being seven on an autumn night.

What I am doing here myself would be
Too boring to tell, though as I wait and wait
I speculate on the ants' activity —

This picture is made up of objectively expressed everyday details.
Another poet would leave the "sodium-illumined street" to do the
work of setting the time of day, but Fuller's "seven on an autumn
night" is, characteristically, even more precise. I value the simplicity
of expression, the vivid detail of this picture and its lack of pretension.
Fuller is more concerned with rendering the scene clearly than with
impressing the reader. This is literally the poem of a man prone, in
Hardy's phrase, "to notice such things". The diction of these lines is
very plain and direct. We find here a straightforward unobfuscated
poetry of things, in which language aims to paint the scene as clearly
as possible, and in which things are allowed an actual life of their own
outside the consciousness of the author. The poem is direct, unfussy
and precise in tone, expressing a clear sense of the everyday, yet in
which observation of the ants, in due course, leads to wider thoughts
on society.

The drug Mianserin enchants. It follows, therefore, that everyday
reality and dream are in as direct conflict in the sonnets as they
were in "At a Warwickshire Mansion". The last Mianserin sonnet is
"Dreams and Art", the final poem in *New and Collected Poems 1934-
84*. Its first line, "Art is to try to impart a narrative/Less boring than
dreams", restates a theme which runs through the following books,
culminating in the 1989 book *Available for Dreams*.

A look at sequences from the three post-1985 books makes it clear
that much of the work published since then can be seen to form
part of one continuous autobiographical poem. The first, *Subsequent
to Summer*, is a book-length sequence of poems which appeared in
1985, the same year as the collected volume. The book consists of a
dedicatory poem, a love poem prelude, then a sequence of forty-nine
unrhymed poems, with a final coda. Each poem (with the exception of
the coda) is fourteen lines in length, each couplet of which is separated
from the next by a space, as it were letting air into, and opening out,
a form otherwise resembling that of the tightly controlled traditional
sonnet. Robert Lowell played a wholly dissimilar variation on the
fourteen lines of the sonnet in his sequence *Notebook* in 1970.

As the title indicates the overall mood of *Subsequent to Summer*
is of a leisurely and meditative autumnal reverie. Themes that recur in the sequence are music, painting, the poet Wallace Stevens,
and the wide range of Fuller's day to day reading, be it of science or

poetry. But the dominant themes are old age, life's small daily pleasures, and the freshness of nature, particularly as seen in the small spiders, insects and birds in his domestic back garden. The motto of the poems might well be "Don't fear the obvious", as Fuller wrote in "Landscapes", a phrase, incidentally, which might have been written by Larkin. The poem includes a spider, a theme which reappears throughout this book and which links it with the bathroom poem, already referred to, beginning "A spider in the bath. The image noted". A spider also appears in no. 20, "Dimensions", which, characteristically, manages in fourteen lines to move from specific beginnings to an abstract conclusion, (respectively a spider and the cosmos):

> The spider, cunningly cocooned all winter
> In a corner of the bathroom, never woke.
>
> One can't help feeling envious in a way.
> The eyrie goes on getting blacker: who
>
> Will dare to pull it down? I read that infants
> On a glass floor will never hesitate
>
> To crawl across a chasm. Shall we thus
> Go into our eternal bathroom coign?
>
> From the same text it seems the cosmos is
> Symmetrical in some fine, abstract sense.
>
> I've never doubted my affinity
> In the natural world with even the grotesque;
>
> Prepared to die in no more dimensions than
> Three bedroom planes, chasms irrelevant.

The poem incorporates a variety of worlds harmoniously: that of the spider — a thing almost too small to notice — through thoughts on the nature of death, to the startling metaphysical image of the child on a glass floor, and the intellectual world of physics, scientific concepts, and the cosmos. The reader is led skilfully and easily between dissimilar things, but there is no sense of the progression from the concrete to the abstract being forced. The poem contains complex concepts but expresses them in a lucid manner, including the death wish in — "One can't help feeling envious in a way" — a line which in its colloquial yet precise tone is instantly recognizable. Fuller's tone — called by Anthony Thwaite, in his poem "For Roy Fuller at Seventy", "The antiseptic note I find so cheering" — effortlessly binds together these disparate things. His tone is by turns personal, measured, emotionally restrained yet warm and welcoming to the reader, buttonholing, polite, wry, ironic, questioning, sane, precise, mellow and meditative. It enables this poem to move easily between various worlds and to focus large concepts into a human dimension.

The theme of the humble spider reappears in a number of other poems leading to similarly broad statements. In "Spinning in October" the poem begins "Wisely the spider spins among the sedum" and ends "I marvel freshly, too,/At the amazing pleasures of the human."; while in "Landscapes" "The spider hesitates before/Stepping from charcoal carpet to oatmeal rug." Both memorable general statements rising quite naturally from the specific roots of an image from the natural world noted.

Fuller's next book *Consolations*, 1987, is divided into four sections: I Age, II Footnotes, III Tenners, IV Seasons. The "Footnotes" section contains the poem, "Strange Revelations", based on a visit to Durham for a poetry reading. The poem mentions Louis Allen, to whom it is dedicated, reviewing books in the TLS on "old Japan". This leads to a stanza wherein Fuller memorably defines his own art in terms of expressing things as they are — rather than as they might be — the better to disenchant and disintoxicate:

> I've always longed to write mysterious works,
> Though conscience, as a rule, compelling me
> To stick to life, my life, and so express
>   Mostly the everyday.

The book contains poems in a wide variety of forms, with one section, "Tenners", consisting of a sequence of thirteen ten-line interrelated poems. The tone of the book differs from *Subsequent to Summer*, but continues themes such as the animal and bird life seen from his garden window, the changing seasons, old age and poor health, the vivid actuality of everyday things, and other poets as in "Old poets":

> Reading old Arthur Symons in the night,
> I wake and find the garden black and white;
> The sky, as he might say,
> A symphony of grey —
> With drums of black and piccolo of white.

The garden here is described through imagery taken from music. The language is pared down and simple, yet the tone is again engagingly personal and leisurely, as in that "old Arthur Symons" and the aside "as he might say". "Strange Revelations" aside, these poems express that mix of everyday life, simple diction, and a deeper "mystery" which we associate with Japanese and Chinese poems in English translation.

Fuller's last book of verse was *Available for Dreams*, published in 1989 and joint winner of the Royal Society of Literature William Heinemann Award for 1990. The book's form returns to the predominately unrhymed fourteen-line form of *Subsequent to Summer*. Its cumulative effects are best experienced when the book is read as a single poem. Many themes already discussed reappear: old age, the life of the garden, the specific sense of the important detail of the everyday world and, especially, the dream theme developed from "Mianserin Sonnets" on. The wide range of Fuller's later poetry is plainly seen in the contrast between dreams and the everyday world which are both central to his work. There is also present a sombre new sense of mortality.

Available for Dreams consists of seven numbered sections, which contain groupings of individual poems and linked, often numbered, sequences such as "Kitchen Sonnets", "Lessons of the Summer", "*Dans un Omnibus de Londres*" and "The Cancer Hospital", this last an autobiographical episode of great force and honesty, which ends the book. As with *Subsequent to Summer* and *Consolations*, the poems continue to balance the various worlds of observed reality, personal feeling and scientific facts. The book's combination of scientific information, intellectual daring and a modest meditative tone brings to my mind the fine and still undervalued sonnets of Alfred Tennyson's elder brother Charles Turner.

"Kitchen Sonnets" consists of a numbered sequence of fourteen sonnets around the central theme of the kitchen of Fuller's Blackheath house. The two words of the title neatly contrast the characteristic "unpoetical" everyday of the kitchen with the mainstream prosodic tradition. Few poets have tried to write sonnets on the kitchen, yet Fuller's ambition to make art, the life of the intellect, the daily life of the garden and other everyday realities cohere in unrhymed sonnets is an undoubted success. An example is number five:

> Things here have taken three score years and ten
> Properly to love — the washing on the line
> Stirred by December English air, mild still;
> Marmalade pot; the partner still alive —

The poem ends on the musical reference, "Abominable tritones linked in diminished sevenths", which is quite different in both imagery and tone, yet which fits quite comfortably in the same poem.

"Lessons of the Summer" is a sequence of sixteen poems. The interweaving of the, by now familiar, late Fuller themes of the various lives of birds and insects, intellectual thought, daily domestic events, and music, make this — to me — a particular personal favourite. The adaptation of the sonnet form is again used with great formal skill to hide rather than reveal its art. The tone is meditative, the rhythms near Robert Frost's idea of "the sound of sense" in their equal mixing of speech and thought, as in number ten:

> Two summer "Pieces for Small Orchestra",
> In boyhood heard on a ten-inch 78,
> Appear in a Beecham disc remastering:
> Exaggerated, my old boast I knew
> Every last note of Delius's score.

The precise and objective manner expresses very clearly a satisfyingly complete poetic personality and, simultaneously, presents an actual world outside the "I" of the poet. In many ways, while Fuller's prose autobiographies give a rounded picture of the narrative of his outer life, the late poems, by focusing on his rich inner life, in fact contain what I see as the essential autobiography. The sequence has a mellow, slightly melancholy, almost Robert Bridges-like cool repose, as in number six:

> The end of summer (and perhaps of cities)
> Presaged by withered grass on tops of walls.
> The heart beats slightly faster on its lattice
> Of bone at suchlike Tennysonian symbols
> This season of the year, ostensibly
> The most removed from mutability.

Each sonnet adds a little more to the mosaic. There is a constant balance between self-consciousness and its opposite, as Fuller alternately addresses lines such as "Can't I elevate/My trousered verse?" apparently directly to the reader, and then adopts a more reflective tone in the lines from number eleven:

> The starlings have started chuntering in the leaves,
> Saying the summer must be past its best.
> A weed's uprooting from the terrace stone
> Brings out some ant eggs which the ants take down,

After uncertain panic, to their nest;
So still the season owns unfinished lives.

A more ornate expression of the objective manner is present here,
but one still allied to Fuller's career-long linguistic fastidiousness. An
increasingly personal tone can be found in a sonnet such as "Teatimes
Past and Present", which mentions a change of heart: "My undemon-
strative/Nature, besides, could never show the love/That unaccount-
ably blossoms in old age". That emotional warmth is present too
in "Postscript", the final poem in the sequence "The Cancer Hospital". This particular poem is all the more moving for its sense of
emotional kinship with friends and his fellow man — something new
from one who described himself, albeit humorously, forty years before
in "Obituary of R. Fuller" as "So unemotional and shy/Such friends
as he retained would cry/With baffled boredom, thankful they/Were
not part of his family." In contrast Roy Fuller now writes "My hands
are burnt through cooking, by roses scarred" and ends the last poem
in the book with fine lines accepting equally mortality, the need for
disenchantment, and acceptance of the imaginative images of friends
relived in dreams:

                    The way is long —
      Shortish for some — and up and down for most.
      Even insomniacs, if tired enough,
      Eventually throw off their wearying load.
      Available for dreams: a mighty cast
      Of all the dead and living of my life.

NOTE

1. Auden, W.H. *The Dyer's Hand* (New York: Random House, 1962) 27.

ALAN BROWNJOHN

The High Style and the Low Style

Probably no living English poet has taken up more constantly than Roy Fuller the themes of the man in the street and the poet in society. He consistently felt himself to be the ordinary man, a member of mass civilisation, with a job (albeit a responsible one, as solicitor to a large building society) which tied him — for forty years — to quotidian matters: "Builders of realms, their tenants for an hour." But as a poet, as an alert and mordantly perceptive observer with an ironic overview of human affairs and a reverence for the "glamour of unapproachable geniuses", he was really rather a special version of the man on the Woolwich omnibus. Much of his verse is about the ambiguities generated when one of these figures takes on the role of the other, and for a good bit of his writing life he seems to have seen himself wavering uneasily between the two. Yet this dilemma was never a disabling one. Fuller's triumph was to have made from it a poetry which has looked outwards from the experiences (including the books and the music) mulled over in reflective solitude, and provided a continuous, highly individual commentary on the malaise of the time.

The characteristic Fuller preoccupations took shape in his poetry very gradually. Most of the work in his very early volumes (he looked for a while like a belated "thirties" poet) is graphically descriptive and immediate: in *The Middle of a War* (1942) things were moving with alarming speed, and there were distinctions to be made between "August 1940" and "October 1940" in poems of those titles. This, in its way, is "social reporting", and Louis MacNeice (who coined the phrase) might have approved the intention, even if he did not influence the style. Fuller's mood seems passively observant, not actively committed or indignant, and not nearly so "dogmatic" as he believed. The reflective note and the muted romanticism suggest the influence of Stephen Spender at least as much as that of W.H. Auden — about whose influence Fuller was so candid as to state how lucky he felt himself to be in falling under it. In 1991, very interestingly, he contributed a poem in ten rhyming couplets to *A Garland for Stephen Spender*, assembled by Barry Humphries for presentation to Spender on his eighty-second birthday. In a footnote Fuller explained that

"With one exception the sources are from Stephen Spender's pre-war poetry, read at the time, remembered ever since."

The kind of war poetry Fuller wrote was especially typical of the Second World War: that of the serviceman left waiting for something to happen, enduring tensions and loneliness either in Britain or in foreign places, seen all the more sharply for the alienation imposed by service routines. Service experience is turned to good account in some excellent poems about Africa in *A Lost Season* (1944). But we have to wait for his first post-war book, *Epitaphs and Occasions* (1949), for the early signs of the later and more familiar Fuller beginning to emerge.

The clues are to be found in the witty octosyllabic couplets of the "Dedicatory Epistle" and the "Obituary of R. Fuller". The views expressed are emphatic, and pointed topical references (including literary references) abound. But a wry sense of limitation is pervasive:

> I might have cut a better figure
> When peace was longer, incomes bigger.
> The 'nineties would have seen me thrive,
> Dyspeptic, bookish, half-alive.
> Even between the wars I might
> With luck have written something bright.

The grandeur of the greatest art ("the Wagner we await") is indubitable and magnetic, even in an age which does not heed it. But it will elude Fuller, in his "small-bourgeois element":

> His infant traumas somewhat worse,
> He would have written better verse.

Creative pursuits come to seem difficult to reconcile with the demands of a more mundane — but also more menacing — world. And yet from this point onwards he steadily expands his technical resources and widens the range of his themes: the poet of limits becomes the poet of a rueful humanist vision for whom man's very inadequacies have their necessity.

From the early nineteen-fifties, when he was wholly settled into his post-war life with job, house and family, Fuller's poetry alternated unexpectedly between a "high" style, in which he achieved genuine power and eloquence, using traditional and challenging verse forms with impressive ease, and a "low" style employed to treat details of everyday living in an engagingly bizarre fashion. The *New and Collected Poems* of 1984, which chooses amply from all the individual books up to *The Reign of Sparrows* (1980) and adds others from most stages of his writing, shows a process which was fascinating to observe in separate volumes as they appeared.

It was *Counterparts* (1954) which brought the first wholly successful poems in the "high" Fuller manner (although in format it was still akin to the well-made little books "produced in complete conformity with the authorized economy standards" during the war). "Rhetoric of a Journey" is perhaps too slow and solemn, and "Translation" only an acceptably neat satire, but the grave cadences of "A Wet Sunday in Spring" show the style:

> The embattled green proliferates like cells.
> I think feebly of man's wrong organizations,
> Incurable leaders, nature lying in wait
> For weakness like an animal or germ,
> And aircraft growling in the summer air.

Mankind is mistaken, pitiable, dangerous and uneasy, and the poet in this society feels both neglected and guilt-ridden. Fuller's rhetoric about his situation is never hollow, but packed with sense. At the same time, enjoying his own precarious security, Fuller finds himself nudged into feeling by the smallest kind of symbolic event, and that produces something else:

> A strange dog trots into the drive, sniffs, turns
> And pees against a mudguard of my car.
> I see this through the window, past *The Times*,
> And drop my toast and impotently glare. . .
>
> And so the entertainment of the morning
> Headlines is temporarily spoiled for me:
> During my coffee I must heed their warning,
> The fate of millions take half seriously.

This poem, "Inaction", is a fine example of his "low" style: here he has become the laureate of the little symbolic disturbances which break the even tenor of living with reminders of different matters: the spider in the bath (which has become his most celebrated image), the lost fountain pen, the feel of the jelly baby ("in its rigid arms/Held close against its side,/And absolute identity with others,/Its pathos and fate reside,/That else had not died.")

None of this, however, prepared Fuller's readers for either the sustained power of the finest poems in his 1957 volume, *Brutus's Orchard*, or the verse experiments of *New Poems* in 1968 — arguably his two best books (although he wrote disconcertingly in 1991 that he regretted "not using rhyme when I wrote a lot of syllabic verse some years ago", as if the tough, intelligent colloquial tone of *New Poems* actually needed rhyme). In an introduction to a 1982 selection of his poems, *The Individual and his Times*, he said of *Brutus's Orchard*: "in a sense all the poems were set in a place where the love for wife and children, and the wish to create, were threatened by tyrants, injustice — and the urgings of conspirators." For Caesar's Rome, then, read the post-war world — or perhaps even post-Suez Britain, with its conviction of a noble past and its dismal sense of impending menace or chaos in the present. The handsome format of *Brutus's Orchard* (no "economy standards" observed: there is almost twice the page area of *Counterparts*) allowed the poems ample room; and they seemed truly to expand, in breadth of outlook and technical confidence, developing ingenious and moving variations within the unity of this theme.

The process can be seen in the flexible pentameters of "The Ides of March" or the succinct couplets of "Pictures of Winter" (for Fuller, poetry is essentially "a succinct art"), in the "Mythological Sonnets" or the chilling quatrains of "Discrepancies":

> Even smooth, feared executives have leisure
> To show the inadequacy of their love . . .

or the sweeping stanzas of "One and Many":

> I read of crises and prepare for living
> In that strict hierarchy of
> A miser body made for giving
> And which prepared for war desiring love.

And the best example is "At a Warwickshire Mansion":

> In the dank garden of the ugly house
> A group of leaden statuary perspires;
> Moss grows between the ideal rumps and paps
> Cast by the dead Victorian; the mouse
> Starves behind massive panels; paths relapse
> Like moral principles; the surrounding shires
> Darken beneath the bombers' crawling wings.
> The terrible simplifiers jerk the strings.

Yeatsian cadences have here been brought on into the 1950s and applied to a changed world by a wholly different poet. Such high points of Fuller's high style deserved more generous recognition than they received, especially as there was little in English poetry to match them at the time, before the Larkin of "The Whitsun Weddings" and "The Building".

The book between *Brutus's Orchard* and *New Poems* is *Buff* (1965), where Fuller relaxes again into a more personal mode, a riddling one in the sequence of thirteen-liners "To X", love poems by a kind of sonnet out of a kind of villanelle, and a weirdly observant one in his "Bagatelles", which look ahead to the sharp laconic comments on day-to-day life, including domestic life, which he assembled in batches (sometimes large batches) in his later volumes. But it's in *New Poems* that he made another venturesome leap into new verse forms. "The springs of verse are flowing after a long/Spell of being bunged up"; and the adoption of the syllable-count is remarkably well-suited to Fuller's sometimes ungainly diction, its occasional blending (in the low style) of almost legal exactness with half-humorous colloquialisms. Poems here like "Heredity" and "Reading *The Bostonians* in Algeciras Bay" show a fully-formed grand manner which is all his own:

> What a mess, societies of men!
> At first spreading out along these coasts,
> Leaving their driftwood and turds afloat,
> Amphorae capsized by sand, pillars
> Broken, democratic orations
> Echoing hollowly to lands of
> Fog . . .

New Poems is a distinguished and varied book, packed with absorbing argument concerning the role of art in human society and the status of the artist. Already there are hints of the autumnal note, which prevails in *From the Joke Shop* (1975) and succeeding volumes, but his later and shorter poems derive authority from the expansiveness of this middle period. Curiously, the most sustained later treatment of its themes comes not in the verse of collections like *Consolations* (1987) but in a return to fiction with the 1991 novel, *Stares*, where a group of "mental rehabilitation" patients confront themselves (the menace of a Middle Eastern crisis with nuclear overtones pressing on their personal lives) through the medium of a staged reading of Chekhov's *The Seagull*. But the poems of his own seventh and eighth decades convert Fuller's tendency to observe tiny moments with self-deprecating humour, to digress, to complain, or make fastidious demands on life, into entertaining — and poignant — art in which the "high" style is never far away, as in "The Gods", from *Available for Dreams* (1989):

> Down the pane, tadpoles chase one another. Burning,
> iced constellations are about to appear,
> and still remoter intimations. A kind
> of comfort comes in reading that even gods
> may not know the universe's origin.

The editor of *The Individual and his Times* (perhaps at Fuller's suggestion) chose to end his selection with a true curiosity of natural history, the lungworm. This creature goes on repeated progresses through the guts of the pig, its eggs hatching during the intervals in the innards of the earthworm. The poem called "Autobiography of a Lungworm" is another from *Brutus's Orchard*:

> I feel, though I am simple, still the whole
>   Is complex; and that life —
> A huge doomed throbbing — has a wiry soul
>   That must escape the knife.

"Wiriness of soul" might aptly describe the persistence and integrity with which this most absorbing of poets explored and interpreted his time and contrived to be, by turns, eloquent and approachably intimate with it.

CHRISTOPHER LEVENSON

Roy Fuller and Syllabic Verse

One wonders how Robert Frost, who once commented that writing
free verse is like playing tennis without the net, would have reacted to
syllabic verse. Syllabics, after all, a system that counts, and arranges
the poem in terms of, the number of syllables in a line rather than the
number of stresses, may restore the net, but for most readers that net
is invisible and, more to the point, inaudible. Or at least seems so,
though the practised reader can in fact *sense* syllabics (as opposed
to simply counting syllables) by a kind of tautness and precision of
statement that at their best syllabics give rise to, much as one can detect a good sonnet by ear long before one has verified that it contains
fourteen lines and a certain rhyme scheme.

Unlike free verse, syllabics has not proved to be one of the major
battlegrounds in the discussion of modern verse. Roy Fuller certainly
came to the skirmish late, most notably in his 1968 volume *New
Poems*: late, but well-armed. What I hope to do here is to outline
first something of the current theory and practice of syllabics prior
to *New Poems*, in the work of Marianne Moore, W.H. Auden and —
since both Roy Fuller and Donald Davie regard her work so highly —
in that of Elizabeth Daryush. (There are of course others, such as
Thom Gunn and George MacBeth, whose use of syllabics would be
interesting to consider, but three will have to do for now.) I will
then look in more detail at Roy Fuller's practice in order to assess its
significance both within and beyond his own oeuvre.

Syllabics seem to have occurred independently both to Marianne
Moore in the United states and to Elizabeth Daryush in England, in
the same year, 1916. Its *raison d'être* is obvious: if one of the main
purposes of art is to eliminate, or at least contain, the arbitrary and
the accidental and to suggest patterns in human experience, the free
verse then in the ascendant needed to be structured if total adhoccery
were to be avoided. Is this not in fact the same motivation that impels
William Carlos Williams many years later to invent the triadic line,
a need to re-introduce some measure, some way of providing aural or
visual parameters?

Not that there has been a great deal of theorizing either on the
need for, or on the practice of, syllabics. Marianne Moore, its most

conspicuous exponent, specifically rejects any regulatory role when she says, as quoted by Fuller in *Owls and Artificers*, concerning the organizing of syllabic verse, "I don't want it artificial and it ought to be continuous. . .I like to have it all natural and consecutive, no matter how it counts upon the page" (*Owls and Artificers* 51). Elsewhere, interviewed by Donald Hall, she speaks of considering the stanza as the unit of syllabic verse, a view exemplified by Auden's practice and specifically endorsed by Fuller in his Oxford lectures. However, in that same lecture Fuller does mildly reprove Marianne Moore for departing from "the foundation of what, though primarily a discipline for the poet, is for the reader authorized by ingenuity and symmetry" (*Owls and Artificers* 48); and he goes on to comment that "it is syllabic verse's extreme formal element that above all else gives one confidence in its validity." (*Owls and Artificers* 64)

Although Fuller's first real involvement with syllabics derived from being asked to review Marianne Moore's *Collected Poems* in 1951, he seems on the whole more at home intellectually with the example and precepts of Elizabeth Daryush, a daughter of Poet Laureate Robert Bridges — himself a great verse experimenter — and the other Founding Mother of Syllabics. Daryush is far more consistent and prescriptive than Marianne Moore, whom incidentally she had hardly read and who thus had very little influence on her own work. This prescriptive quality may be seen in her remarks from a letter to him quoted by Fuller in his Oxford Lectures, about the mere counting of syllables being a very small part of what is needed in syllabic verse:

> . . . it seems often forgotten that mere permissiveness does not in itself make a new art form. It must be supported by other, counterpointing, disciplines, the more difficult because self-imposed. . . Since power and style depend upon the enhancing of sense and feeling by the form and emphasis of the metre, and since, perhaps, the most important emphasis is on the last word of the line, this becomes a throne, often spotlighted by rhyme, and its occupant must be carefully chosen. . .emphasis. . .has to be built up by a subtle internal accord of sense, feeling, grammar and music. (*Owls and Artificers* 67)

Other remarks of hers suggest an at times almost stifling preoccupation with the kinds of rhyme and half rhyme desirable in syllabic verse, though this is matched by Fuller's own detailed discussion of feminine line endings and end-stopping. According to Daryush, rhyme, though not essential to syllabics, is very helpful. She is also quoted as warning against elisions in words such as "heaven" or "flower", since any ambiguity as to how one counts specific syllables is fatal to syllabic verse.

In those last two respects at least, rhyme and elision, Fuller does not follow her example; indeed, he notes that neither Marianne Moore nor Auden "avoid writing in lines of an even number of syllables" (*Owls and Artificers* 54), which tends in his view to the restoration of an iambic metre. This is even truer of the "syllabic sonnet", "Still-life", by Daryush — my own scepticism here is signalled by the inverted commas — that Donald Davie so praises in his introduction to Daryush's *Collected Poems*. Whatever its other merits, and it has several, one could be forgiven, I think, for reading the following eight lines and not realizing that they are intended as syllabics:

> Through the open French window the warm sun
> lights up the polished breakfast table, laid
> round a bowl of crimson roses, for one —
> a service of Worcester porcelain, arrayed
> near it a melon, peaches, figs, small hot
> rolls in a napkin, fairy rack of toast,
> butter in ice, high silver coffee-pot,
> and, heaped on a silver salver, the morning's post.

In most of Fuller's own syllabic stanzas odd numbers of syllables predominate, and he specifically advocated eleven syllable lines behind which, he said, "its the ghost of the iambic pentameter, but the constant intrusion of just one extra syllable — the exercise of accommodating it — removes the sense there is about blank verse that its possibilities of variation have already been exhausted, or at any rate discovered, by the great practitioners of the past." (*Owls and Artificers* 57)

Fuller's own apologia for syllabics ultimately seems closer in spirit to the practice of Moore and Auden than to that of Daryush. As he puts it in the Oxford Lectures, "The use of [syllabics]. . .if not dictated by mere fashion, must reside in providing an escape from iambic cliches, a chance of making fresh music. From the poet's point of view I can testify the techniques can provide a way into the composition of the poem especially by freeing him from the preliminary need to hear his subject, his donnée, his initial observation or image, as song — or at least the often elusive song of traditional stress metre." (*Owls and Artificers* 54) The reference to "fresh music" is perhaps a little misleading, especially when juxtaposed with the later sentence that argues for freedom from conventional "song", and Fuller's own syllabic poems, even at their most impressive, are not musical. Indeed he seems to recognize this when, earlier on, he speaks of Marianne Moore as very often writing "not prose or the prose poem but poetry with prose's rhetoric, complexity and ease, poetry without adventitious musical aid, whose units are arguments and paragraphs." (*Owls and Artificers* 50) And if for Moore the general viability of syllabics was in the convenience with which she could incorporate "extracts from prose works into her poetry" (*Owls and Artificers* 53), Fuller was happy to confess a similar python-like ingestion of extracts from Henry James's prose into one of his own poems, "Reading *The Bostonians* in Algeciras Bay", as being part of the process that led to his own experiments in syllabics.

In the case of that other major practitioner of syllabics, W.H. Auden, whose first essays in this form date from 1939 and 1940, it is interesting to note that, according to George T. Wright, in discovering "the perfect suitability of syllabics to the poem expressive of quiet personal concern",[1] he finds at the same time an antidote to the more pretentiously prophetic note that had characterized many of his more public Thirties poems. Take these lines from near the beginning of "In Praise of Limestone":

> What could be more like Mother or a fitter background
> 　　For her son, the flirtatious male who lounges
> Against a rock in the sunlight, never doubting
> 　　That for all his faults he is loved; whose works are but
> Extensions of his power to charm? From weathered outcrop
> 　　To hill-top temple, from appearing waters to
> Conspicuous fountains, from a wild to a formal vineyard,
> 　　Are ingenious but short steps that a child's wish
> To receive more attention than his brothers, whether
> 　　By pleasing or teasing, can easily take.

Here, as in other major poems from the later volumes, "Thanksgiving for a Habitat" and parts of "Bucolics" and "Horae Canonicae", the syllabic verse, in Wright's view, "has something of the same effect as the surprising syntax and changing tone colour: one line may suggest one metre, but the next matching line will contradict it. Again the point is to forestall the too complacent participation of the reader; it is also to suggest the extent of the speaker's casualness: no rigid metre for *his* talk, but a liquid flow of the language. Just as the syntax and the tone must never fall into obvious patterns, the syllables must never accidentally, for more than about a line, fall into some accentual pattern. The skill is in endlessly varying the design, the triple design of metre, sentence and feeling."[2]

Interestingly, although Fuller praised Daryush, despite her ten-syllable lines, while amiably disparaging Auden's later style and warning against its tendency to "greater complexity of diction" (*Owls and Artificers* 59), it was in fact Auden and Moore rather than Daryush whom he followed in most of his practice.

Let us take a closer look now at some of the *New Poems*. Simply as shapes on the page — and as I hope to show this is not a frivolous criterion — most of these poems seem uniform and indeed for the most part they are. The most frequent line lengths are nine or eleven syllables and roughly half of those not arranged as verse paragraphs appear in four to seven line stanzas. Relatively few stand out by virtue of their distinctive shape. Two that do are "Goddess" and "My dead brothers", both of which employ the same unrhymed quatrain of 11:11:7:7 syllables. As is the case with, say, Marvell's "Horatian Ode", for instance, this form visually draws attention to itself through the marked differences in line length; and, if only because the reader's first, visually alerted assumptions about the presence of rhyme and metrical scheme are frustrated, he or she is thus more attuned to the possibility of different techniques.

One thing that these two poems prove is that, although governed by syllable counts, the line breaks in syllabic verse can be no less crucial than in regular metrical forms; not, it is true, in terms of cadence and counterpoint but certainly in terms of sense emphasis. Thus the initial word of a new line often creates an effect of very deliberate placing. "My Dead Brothers" contains several instances of this, such as

> Later recalled those two dead
> *Babes*, their lives measured in days

or again

> To die before my mother and father was
> *Your* legendary fate, my own to prove so
> *Unconsolatory*. . .

(Italics added)

At other times a comparable effect, concluding the first stanza of "Goddess", seems gratuitous, drawing a surely unneeded attention to the word "all" in

> But what other point, after
> All, had her startling entry?

Such an effect is heightened when the line lengths themselves vary,
in that the reader feels required to look, vainly in this instance, for
some extra meaning in the emphasized phrase "after/All". However,
what in this poem strikes me as an unfortunate, because distracting,
emphasis is more than made up for by the poem's concluding stanza,
where the words "Acting" and "Luck" both receive entirely appropriate and happy emphasis of the kind that substantiates a tone of
voice, an assured intellectual discrimination, which tends in fact to
be one of the dominant tones of syllabic verse.

The same points might be made in relation to the five-line stanzas
of another rather late-Audenesque poem, "The Visitors", where different syllable counts — in this case 11:11:11:11:7 — are clearly visible
on the page, as here in the fourth stanza for instance:

> And the tragedies of our infancy, a
> Degree more real than the howl of the guilty
> King, we rehearse till our death. No wonder They
> Visit us sometimes to remind us of our
> Right to be blessed and consoled.

In "Strange Child", on the other hand, the absence of clearly defined
stanzas, accompanied by syllable counts that fluctuate between ten
and fifteen, throws the reader off and leaves one wondering how much
of a pattern is really intended.

Sometimes, it seems to me, Fuller falls between two styles. This is
the case with two sonnets "Road Safety" and "Mind to Body". The
latter especially, attractive though it is in its imagery, in its attitudes,
in *what* it is saying, seems to fluctuate dangerously:

> Awake already, can't you sleep again?
> Strange body, how you fail to serve the mind
> That wishes above all to be the puissant prince
> Of sensual indolent extremities!
> I see your legs emerging from the rich
> Humus of dreams, in some way anxious for
> Frustrated action, botched creativity,
> In a dawn inhabited only by moths and owls.
>
> At times of physical pain one is convinced
> That what is happening is happening to
> Another body — that merely passing chance
> Has hooked up the throbbing circuit to one's own
> Perception. Likely to be a sad affair,
> Lean flesh, our final reconciliation.

The first two lines are pure iambic, the third contains six iambic feet, while these are followed by three iambic pentameter lines before returning in the seventh line to eleven syllables that are again regularly iambic up to the last word, "creativity" — though even here, by slurring over the second syllable of the word "action", one can make a non-conforming iambic line of it. Line 8, however, has thirteen syllables and is virtually unscannable. And the sestet is similarly erratic: though lines 9 and 10, by virtue of slight elisions — reading "physical" and "happening" as two syllables each — can easily be read as iambic pentameters, lines 11 through 14 all have eleven irreducible syllables.

Why should all this matter? The trouble, surely, arises from mutually exclusive metrical expectations, for, despite Elizabeth Daryush's example, a sonnet in syllabics strikes me at least as a contradiction in terms. Traditionally the sonnet form has implied, and attempted to exemplify, a sense of balance, a rounding out and reconciliation of opposites. Although one might claim that Fuller is deliberately undermining the sonnet form here in order to imitate, to enact, the disruptive effect of the body on the mind's equanimity, such an interpretation seems rather far-fetched in terms of what the poem as a whole seems to be saying, even in its very last phrase, "our final reconciliation". What I am suggesting is that, while poets such as Hopkins, or in a very different and less important way, E.E. Cummings, expand the sonnet's metrical resources, their innovations are consistent within themselves. Whereas, as Fuller himself observes, "as twelve tone music must avoid the old concord, so. . . syllabics must in general avoid regular stress, certainly any stress pattern that calls attention to itself. . . " (*Owls and Artificers* 56) Here the deviations from the strict sonnet form seem arbitrary and accidental and so benefit neither the accumulated corpus of the sonnet as form nor the rival claims of syllabic verse.

For it is surely the effort involved in conforming to an arbitrarily devised pattern that makes the language of such poetry memorable, the sense that the reader has that vocabulary and sound have been *wrought*. In his responses to a questionnaire in a special issue of *Agenda* magazine devoted to Rhyme, Fuller speaks of being "pro-rhyme, pro-regular metre (to such an extent that nowadays I can hardly bear verse which has not got at least, in Eliot's phrase, the ghost of some metre lurking behind the arras)"; but he adds "it has to be admitted that the poet, myself anyway, must work to make them 'natural' i.e. as uncontrived and as appropriately colloquial as if the discipline were absent."[3] If in one sense there are few poets writing today who would disagree with Fuller about a natural tone of voice, the problem remains that one must make the natural memorable, while memorability in turn derives surely from one's sense that language has been carefully chosen, even though often not chosen at a conscious, intellectual level. The words may well select themselves by processes that elude final analysis; but if they do indeed seem to be "the right words in the right order" this will be because all the resources of language such as imagery, symbol, cadence, internal rhyme, assonance and word music are working in the same direction, centripetally, rather than at cross-purposes. Much of the *effort* of poetry involves precisely this, creating contexts where the poet or his persona can be simple, direct and natural. Affirmations such as Yeats's

> An aged man is but a paltry thing,
> A tattered coat upon a stick, unless
> Soul clap its hands and sing, and louder sing
> For every tatter of its mortal dress . . .

are impressive because, although so simple and direct, we feel that they have been forced out by circumstances that have been evoked or implied or at least made credible by the texture of the surrounding verse. Simplicity is a very volatile quality, with often a very thin line separating the solemn from the bathetic and pompous.

Syllabic verse, because, as Fuller pointed out, it transcends the clichés of the iambic line and its regular metrical expectations, can achieve structures that are both simple and formal. The way in which, as we have seen, it can absorb prose quotations is one indication of this. But by the same token it can also accommodate latinate and polysyllabic language that would otherwise be metrically impossible. Thus in "Romance" we find:

> Only the inspiration may be lacking,
> Not your worthiness — for the preponderance
> Of evidence favours the viability
> Of even chinless countenances. . .

Moreover the rhythmic elasticity of syllabics perhaps also encourages the same kind of dandified, over-exact language — "oblate" as an adjective or "pulchritude" — that occasionally mars the narrative in the autobiographies. Less inherent in syllabic verse is the kind of syntactic inversion that one encounters at times in lines like these that conclude "The Art of the Apple":

> One finds suspiciously
> Romantic the concept now.

Again, though, one might argue from the evidence of the autobiographies (though not from the much more consistently colloquial Oxford lectures) that such vocabulary and such inversions are indeed part of Fuller's *natural* voice. Donald Davie does indeed make a similar, though in my view unconvincing, case for Elizabeth Daryush's diction. Clearly, one person's nature is another person's artifice.

Against these minor dissatisfactions, however, we must set such real triumphs of tone, formal but personal, measured but direct, as we find in "Heredity", which again deserves to be quoted in full:

> Mother, it was this, then, you suffered from in
> The days of my uncaring adolescence —
> This unpleasant and chronic but curable,
> It's said, imbalance of metabolism.
>
> How it would have distressed you to discover
> That with your timid heart you'd also passed on
> A gland too officious, since only the nice
> Lessons of life were to be learnt in your school.
>
> You'd have foolishly liked to bear my symptoms
> As well, to save me the trouble, just as now
> (Though with rather less theoretical risk)
> I'd prefer to have been the unlucky one.
>
> Widowed, lacking the consolations of art,
> How did you stand the long years of uncertain
> Diagnosis, the ineffective drugs, and
> Lastly the blundering knife of that epoch?
>
> Well, you survived. And death was still a decade
> Away. When it came, I was then fully seised
> Of its threat, its grip, its method of bringing
> Itself into life, premature grave-breath, bones —
>
> Closer myself to the state of receiving
> It. But how far then compared with the present!
> Strange we should each get our wish to endure for
> The other; or must the same blood expect to?

Once more we observe the felicitous line breaks — the fastidious distancing of the word "It" (death) in the last stanza, the pause just before "diagnosis" that seems to enact the idea of uncertainty. But what the poem above all exemplifies is the advantage to syllabic verse of some kind of regularity not simply of line lengths (here they are all eleven syllables) but also of stanza form. For no less than is the case with regular metrics, a syllabic poem has to set up some kind of norm if it is ever to achieve tension or surprise.

Ultimately, syllabics can be seen as representing a conservative revolution in a way that Williams's experiments with the triadic line do not, for syllabics tend to restore and reinforce, rather than undermine and fracture, traditional syntax and sentence structures. To that extent Fuller's exploitation of syllabics is of a piece with his overall tendencies that are evident again in such later poems as "On the Demolition in 1980 of the Roxy, Old Dover Road S.E.3" or "Mackerel in the Athenaeum"; the latter especially, with its frequent elisions, reading like a consciously freed up traditional verse form rather than programmatic syllabics. For, despite the occasional almost exotic-sounding slang and vulgarisms, and thanks perhaps increasingly to the influence of his syllabic practice, the general level of his diction and the meticulousness of his sentence and stanza structures, while certainly not "literary" in any limiting traditional sense, nonetheless preserve what one might term a controlled informality.

NOTES

Unless otherwise indicated, all prose quotations are from *Owls and Artificers* by Roy Fuller (London: Deutsch, 1981).

1. Wright, G.T. *W.H. Auden* (New York: Twayne, 1969) 145.
2. Wright, G.T. *W.H. Auden*, 145.
3. Fuller, R. Contribution to "A Survey on Rhyme", *Agenda* 28,4 (Winter 1991) 16–17.

NEIL POWELL

An Aquarian Talent

Astrology, like passive suffering, is not a theme for poetry, but perhaps it may be permitted a fleeting and not altogether solemn appearance in this volume. Some years ago I pinched, or had pressed upon me by an amused and presumably unsober companion in a pub, a beer-mat which thus defines the characteristics—I hesitate to call them qualities—of those of us born beneath the sign of Aquarius. "Sensitive and intellectual," it says, "unconventional and even eccentric. Aquarians are rarely conformists." But of course (who am I trying to kid?) they are qualities: why else would I have kept a cardboard beer-mat for perhaps twenty years? And I've every right to claim them, for I was born on 11 February.

So, in a remoter year, 1912, was Roy Fuller; and on the same day in another year, 1963, Sylvia Plath died. Thus the poetic omens— as, naturally, you'd expect from Aquarian omens of any sort—are contradictory, to say the least. That birthday coincidence drew me to Roy Fuller's work while I was still a schoolboy, as did a second coincidence, or simple stroke of good luck: the informed interest (nothing exceptional, I thought then, but how wrong I was) in contemporary poetry of Alan Hurd, a brilliant English teacher at Sevenoaks School. Alan had an engaging, and highly effective, habit of jotting urgent, cryptic suggestions for further reading on the ends of essays, on bookmarks, on postcards. "What is C. Tomlinson up to?" enquired one; and another, more imperiously, said, "You should read R. Fuller." In conversation a little later—I was probably borrowing Alan's copy of the first Fuller *Collected Poems* (1962)—I remember him mentioning a local connection: something to do with Westerham, he thought.

He was right. During the war, the headquarters of the Woolwich Equitable Building Society had been evacuated from its eponymous South London base to Westerham, which was or became the home of its General Manager, subsequently Chairman, Sandy Meikle. The third in my cluster of coincidences occurred when Sandy and Peggy Meikle moved the three miles from Westerham to become close neighbours of my parents in the somewhat undistinguished West Kent village of Sundridge. A little later—I was by now a student starting postgraduate research on modern poetry—Sandy suggested that I might like to meet the Society's Legal Director, whom he believed was a rather fine poet (not that he, Sandy, knew much about poetry, etc.). That chain of events, with its meshing of chronological and geographical accidents to create an unexpected literary occasion, itself has something pleasingly Fullerish about it.

Sandy, a man who relished honours with an impenetrable blend of delighted self-parody and childlike pride, often seemed to take as much pleasure in being President of the Westerham Amateur Dramatic Society as in being Chairman of the Woolwich. The chance of getting the Oxford Professor of Poetry to give a reading for the WADS wasn't one he could resist; accordingly, an oddly assorted bunch of local worthies assembled at The Crown (an adequate but neither over-exciting nor over-priced restaurant, true to Sandy's style) to meet the great man over a meal before the reading. I've a suspicion I did my best to monopolise his attention, and can only plead that at least I wanted to talk about poetry (and felt, rightly, that this was why I'd been invited); we discussed Yvor Winters, the plain style, the peculiarities of poetic professors.

I can't remember exactly which poems he read to that most difficult of audiences — whose view of poetry must have ranged from the passionately interested to the frankly disapproving — but know that he included one or two pieces of a directness to appeal beyond the "poetry audience" ("Obituary of R. Fuller" perhaps, "Autobiography of a Lungworm" certainly) as well as some of the more weighty and allusive poems which are among his finest of the fifties and sixties — "The Ides of March", "Orders". It's a reassuring thought that, even though he was almost sixty then, so much of his best poetry was still to come.

After the reading, I persuaded Roy and Kate Fuller to stop for a drink at my parents' house; they politely connived at the fiction that it was on their way home. My ulterior motive, not impossibly dishonourable, was to get Roy Fuller to contribute to the "Poetry 1970" survey I was putting together for the little magazine *Tracks*, which I edited. He did, of course, and his comments on the (then) current state of poetry were characteristically wry. Looking back at them over twenty years later, I'm struck by the disconcerting suspicion that much the same could be said today. He would have to replace Ian Hamilton and *The Review* by Michael Schmidt and *P N Review*, but Alan Ross and *London Magazine* would still earn their praise; and his concluding hopes that "the greater interest in poetry will ally itself to better taste and skill" and that "English poetry will extend the *English* tradition, not follow some bastard mid-Atlantic mode" would still, perhaps, be hopes.

The old buffer's growl in that last remark is, of course, something which Fuller fans recognise as a strategy, without always satisfactorily answering the question "Strategy for *what?*" In one of a sequence of poems called "In His Sixty-Fifth Year", he writes:

> Of all my portraits I say: poor likeness.
> 'Colonel (Retired)' or 'Disgusted' stares out. . .

And a few lines later he both acknowledges and excuses

> Reactionary views, advanced mostly
> To raise a laugh — taken as gospel!

That's too easy an escape-route, as Fuller knew and the flailing exclamation-mark mournfully admits: far from being there simply "To raise a laugh", a quirky assortment of "Reactionary views" (ranging, in his last set of memoirs, from a fondness for old, good suits to a detestation of Arts Council-funded community art and BBC permissiveness) was for years a serious element in a complex intellectual personality. No less serious an element is his enduring sense of social humanism. At best, the two coexist in creative tension, or even merge disconcertingly into each other, as here (he's writing of the 1986 Building Societies Act): "As with so many things in one's lifetime — bread, schooling, dress, manners — the enviable friendly society status, invention by British genius of a fair institution for spreading home ownership, was laid open for destruction" (*Spanner and Pen* 77). Some readers may need a quick double-take to perceive that this blimpish grumble is actually an attack on Thatcherite Conservative principles (or lack of them) and a defence of the institution he joined as a young socialist.

A problem here is that cultural judgements made in a specific political context can come to seem askew as the context alters. When Fuller resigned from the Arts Council in 1977, I remember feeling broadly sympathetic towards his stand against jokey junk art: that was before a decade of insufferable middlebrow philistinism in government attitudes to the arts, of mean-spirited ignorance and prejudice directed by advocates of "market forces" against cultural minorities. So, when he repeated in *Spanner and Pen* his attack on community art and his glee at getting subsidy withdrawn from "a fairly dubious magazine" (*Spanner and Pen* 123), it was hard not to feel at least mildly unhappy; and when he wrote, quoting a 1978 memorandum of his own, "I do not believe we have a multicultural society in this country, and I hope we never have" (*Spanner and Pen* 131) mild unhappiness gave way to despair (and a wish to point out that, on the contrary, Britain has had a multi-cultural society since the Roman invasion and is all the better for it). Similarly, in his skirmishes at the BBC, his wish to sustain cultural standards seemed to have tilted too often into wilful censoriousness.

In writing this I worry, though only for a moment, about the occasion: such dissenting notes in a memorial volume? Yes, because that, to propose one of several answers to my earlier question, is a part of what Fuller's strategy is about: to provoke the rest of us into thinking for ourselves and speaking our minds; his highest praise, in *Spanner and Pen*, was reserved for those who enjoy articulate disagreement.

Prose tempted Fuller, despite his sometimes ornate solicitorial hedging, to gestures of apparently combative certainty which would upset the finer balances of the poems. And the poems, especially in what we might crudely define as the second half of his career — that is, since *Collected Poems* (1962) — are finely balanced in ways which seem to have eluded those readers who still undervalue him. *Buff* (1965) provides the enigmatic prelude to this impressive body of work: framed by two sonnet-sequences, "To X" and "The Historian", the book explores fictional and fictionalised themes — and should make Andrew Motion blush to see himself recently described as "the founder of the modern Narrative School", an institution already well-established by the family firm of Fuller & Son. But the decisive change, deliberately signalled though perhaps more momentous than the author himself knew, comes with *New Poems* (1968). Partly the transition is technical, into unrhymed syllabics: a potentially perilous form, as Fuller has himself noted, but one which works extremely well for him. Not only do syllabics suit, as one might expect, the rational, discursive subject-matter of these poems; they also acquire here a far less predictable resonance. In "Orders", the syllabic elevens often sound like unusually ruminative, suspended pentameters as Fuller moves in a graceful intellectual arc from the birds in his garden through Goethe and J.B. Bury, war and poetry, round to this unashamedly rhetorical conclusion:

> And what if ourselves became divine, and fell
> On the pitiful but attractive human,
> Taking the temporary guise of a swan
> Or a serpent: could we return to our more
> Abstract designs untouched by the temporal;
> Would we not afterwards try to get back those
> Beautiful offspring, so mortal, so fated?

It's the scope, as well as the ease of modulation within that scope, which impresses: from here on, indeed, the predominant strand in Fuller's poetry becomes a kind of diary in which the everyday, the cultural, the philosophical exist in complex and *continual* juxtaposition — an effect most strikingly evident in the collection of sixty-three poems in triplets, *From the Joke Shop* (1975), and in the sonnet collection, *Available for Dreams* (1989), essentially its sequel.

Other poets with a supposedly strong line in social observation — Philip Larkin, for instance — take occasional snapshots and then scurry off like spiders to the corners of their webs, waiting gloomily for something else to turn up. Fuller was not at all like that. For him, everyday life was poetic life, a continually evolving and refocusing process and, despite the inevitably increasing number of poems about illnesses and the deaths of friends, a celebratory process too. In a daft moment, I had an image of Roy Fuller making out a sort of shopping-list called "Good things", which went something like: "Blackbirds; M&S sausages; Debussy; 1964 Daimler; Debenham & Freebody (Plymouth); Boiled potatoes (in their jackets); Sparrows; Punk vegetarians; Ella Fitzgerald. . . ". And so on. The apparently lunatic diversity is an asset, of course: the man was incurably hooked on the worthwhile things of life. This love (not too strong a word) of things which make up the tightly woven fabric of his cultural and domestic life could provoke him in prose to furious anger at the prospect of their passing, and in poetry to an exact balance of resilience and tenderness, as in "Images":

> The creeper knows when it must start to blush.
> As in a 'magic' painting-book, the hose
> Reveals an unsuspected spider's web.
> Summer's about to end: let's hope to be
> Inspired by rotten weather, like Debussy.

There are a lot of endings in Roy Fuller, in both senses: poems about ends, ends of poems — the latter, one might reasonably suppose, an obvious consequence of their being so numerous and usually so short. But there's more to it than that. He was in a precise sense a musical poet: one for whom music was a preoccupation and a model, so that his poems are invariably negotiations with cadences, especially the disrupted or teasingly disturbed cadences of the early twentieth-century composers to whom he constantly returns and whose echoes constantly inform his writing. And music, even at its most desolate, is the most mysteriously consoling of the arts, conjuring regenerated hope out of the bleakest conclusions, as Fuller does too in "Programme Notes":

> Relentless minor: how can one disagree
> In rotten times like these? The movements share
> Exceptionally a single tonality.
> But in a piece for four string players there
> Seems to be always mystery in the vibrating air.

It's hard not to sound at least a touch over-sententious in attempting to sum up the astonishing achievement of Fuller's later poems. They are, I think, simply our best record of what it has been like for a cultivated, humane and superbly observant man to live in England in "rotten times like these": exasperation balanced by affection, despair by hope, recorded by an eye which is unflinching, unsparing but seldom unamused. Answer enough, surely, to the question "Strategy for *what?*", and affirmation of the claim Fuller made for himself, though self-deprecatingly of course, at the end of the first sequence from which I quoted here, "In His Sixty-Fifth Year":

> And why so ego-centred the content ?
> Emblematic, I try to persuade myself,
> Of the entire human condition —
> Composers who die in usual pain,
> Who drown, meaning to rescue their wives,
> Regular soldiers, rain-moulded dancers,
> Work of joy and disappointment,
> Life of creativeness and bereavement. . .
> Peering at some enigmatic blot,
> Groping for my glasses in the night-time.

An Aquarian poet? "Sensitive and intellectual" certainly, but "unconventional and even eccentric"? In *Spanner and Pen*, Fuller recounted the story of his joining the BBC Board of Governors at the same time as a businessman, Tony Morgan. Ian Trethowan, he recalled, instantly thought he knew which was which: "the long-haired, trendily dressed chap was the poet, Roy Fuller; the businessman was the short-haired, cropped-moustached, conventionally garbed other" (*Spanner and Pen* 116). Everyone knows, of course, that poets are a weird bunch. But to be a major poet while pretending to be — no, being — a retired suburban solicitor must be the most subversively eccentric trick of all. Only an Aquarian could have pulled it off.

NOTE

All prose quotations are from *Spanner and Pen* by Roy Fuller (London: Sinclair-Stephenson, 1991).

A.T. TOLLEY

Fuller's Earth:
Delving into the Notebooks

The best basis for the study of the composition of poetry would be to have before one all the drafts and notes made in the composition of a variety of poems by a variety of poets. This desideratum might seem fairly easy to attain. In fact, it is not. In particular, the number of poets who have bequeathed to us all, or nearly all, their poetic worksheets in an orderly form is very small. Roy Fuller was such a poet. Almost all his notebooks, meticulously kept, are to be found in the Brotherton Collection at the University of Leeds; and the complete drafting of almost all his poems is to be found in those notebooks.

The first of the books comes from the early years of World War II, when Fuller was in the Navy. The series runs from October 1941 almost to the present, with a gap from December 1945 to November 1955. This gap is partly filled by a notebook donated to the Lockwood Memorial Library at the State University of New York at Buffalo; and by a notebook in the Arts Council Collection of Modern Literary Manuscripts in the British Library (BM Add MS 52618), which contains poems from June 1954 to November 1955. There are twenty-five notebooks at Leeds, varying from small pocket notebooks with spiral bindings, to a leather bound volume with "John Donne" on the spine — a mock-up for a binding of the Nonesuch *John Donne*. After 1963, Fuller regularly used such binder mock-ups; and many of the volumes are very attractive. Most of them contain an analytic summary of their contents at the end, where Fuller frequently shows in what periodicals the poems have been published and works out which poems are to be used in his next book. Very few poems have not been collected. The notebooks contain drafting of both his regular poems and his poems for children; though the latter are largely drafted in independent volumes.

The mode of procedure seems to have remained the same throughout Fuller's career. A poem will almost always begin with what is to be, and remain, its first line. It will be drafted line by line, usually in the poetic form that it is eventually to have, and frequently from start to finish in the first draft. In many cases, each line of the draft will correspond to a line in the final poem; though in some cases there has been rejection of whole sections. However, the lines themselves may be modified — possibly several lines in sequence; and there is considerable modification of word and phrase.

Some modification is made to achieve a better choice of word or to eliminate a redundant phrase; other, to fit the metre or to answer the needs of rhyme. In certain sonnets, particularly some of the later "Mianserin Sonnets", there is considerable juggling with phrases to fit the form without loss of other effects; but in most poems, particularly the earlier ones, the rhymes appear as the lines are written. This is not the case with some other poets: with them, the poem may be drafted and then modified to fit the rhyme pattern; or the rhyme itself may seem to lead the poet into finding his phrases. One does not have the sense that either is the case with Fuller.

Most of Fuller's poems have gone through two, three, four or even five drafts, depending on the complexity of form. Some famous early ones, such as "Spring 1942" ("One evening we were sitting by") came very easily in as little as two drafts. When completed, poems were dated; though Fuller sometimes came back for a further revision and appended a later date. Poems were, however, seldom taken to completion without interruption. A new poem (or two or more) will generally intervene, its drafting interspersed with that of the earlier poem. Fuller made very few notes to himself, and there is little extraneous material; though the books contain addresses to which they may be returned.

The most notable impression made by the notebooks (apart from their general neatness) is that of Fuller's great fluency. Few poets get the pattern of a poem in such detail at the first go. A good example is "Thirty Years On" (from 1973) — a poem occasioned by taking down his copy of Francis Scarfe's book of 1942, *Auden and After* (because he was writing something about Kenneth Allott) only to be reminded that his mother gave him the book. The mixture of narrative and reflection, of course, gives to the poem a fairly obvious structure easily arrived at by Fuller. There is no rhyme pattern, the form being merely a division into three line sections, the effective, unarbitrary use of which undoubtedly required a care that is effectively hidden in the end result. The poem was completed in three drafts, but returned to later. There is little imagery, apart from the details of the event described, and not much overtly figurative use of language. A precision of phrase, a careful manipulation of tone and speech rhythm, are what gives the poem its power.

Fuller's fluency is seen in the fact that twenty-two lines of the first draft of this forty-two line poem survive in the printed version with very little alteration, some lines remaining completely unchanged. It is on the poem's conclusion that Fuller expends the most pains — a quite frequent pattern in his writing. He seems possibly to have come to a halt after thirty lines, as he appends a marginal note to himself, "severe winter of '42 — Willie"; which is followed by a further note "Willie shoe brushes". The reference is to his by then dead wartime friend, Willie Robertson (mentioned in the third volume of Fuller's autobiography, *Home and Dry*) whose shoe brushes he still had and used. Willie Robertson appears in the later stanzas of the first draft, but disappears in the second draft, presumably because the memory of him was perceived not to be germane to the general emotional movement of the poem. At its end, the first draft contains a hint of the reference to Fuller's father that was to provide the conclusion to the poem; but in this first version the poem peters out.

In the second version, a note to himself "Did I thank properly? Can't now" seems to show a clarification of focus of the poem in terms of his relation to his mother. There is some difficulty in accommodating to the form the description of his father's fascination with his mother's manner of holding her pen; but very little else is altered in this draft, except in the three lines concerning his not adequately thanking his mother — the emotional turning point of the poem, where there is still some problem in articulating feeling. The third draft is a copying out (with a few alterations) of the second draft to make a "final version", which is dated 15.ix.73. The only redrafting of note here is, significantly, a return to the lines about thanking his mother.

However, Fuller came back to the poem, making further alterations, this time in passages that seem not to have troubled him before. The statement that Allott "Had said what his talent was to let him say" is softened to the (possibly less natural) "Had uttered what the grudging genius/Of verse was to permit"; and a similar softening occurs in the reference to his father "Dead in his youth", where "Dead" is in a forcefully assertive position at the beginning of a section. It becomes "My father, before his youthful death". In the printed version, the autobiographically factual "radar sets, in huts/Unheated" is replaced by "A Whitmanesque night passage through the camp;/Ratings with branches, bottles: all dead drunk", where the explicit reference to Christmas reaches back to the memory of the gift that prompted the poem; though Whitman seems arguably less in place than the unheated huts.

The mode of drafting, in which, on each occasion, the poem is written out in full, even though there is little change from version to version, is characteristic of Fuller. No doubt this is related to the principal effects cultivated in the poem (and in his poetry generally): tone and variation of tone; a sense of voice and change of voice — features that depend on the movement of the poem as a whole rather than on local effects. There is little figurative use of language that draws attention to itself; and what images there are in the poem arise naturally from the incidents of the poem. The reference to his being in "darkest Africa" (which replaces in the printed version a reference to his being in the "Fleet Air Arm") is not part of an overall orchestration of imagery, but comes across as a slightly self-deflative use of the customary cliche.

In the case of many poems, the modifications can almost be regarded as a process of fine tuning. What seemed in most of his drafting to demand work was, as already noted, finding rhymes in complex forms. In poems such as "The End of a Leave", the majority of the poem came easily: by the second draft the first two stanzas of this three-stanza poem were as printed. The reworking was around the conclusion and its focusing image:

"Leave Taking at the Station"

Out of this damp black light
The noise of locomotives
A thousand whispering,
Sharp-nailed
~~Delicate~~, sinewed, slight
I meet that alien thing
Your hand, with all its motives.

Far from the roof of night
And iron these encounter
In the   gigantic hall
                 widening bodies
Out of our ~~human, small~~   light between us
                 human, small
These hands exchange their counters

~~Our relation becomes too simple~~
And our relation now
Grows
~~Are~~   terrifyingly simple
         our
Like   hands in this city
         our
Against ~~the~~ times, this hour
Of parting

> Suddenly our relation
> Is
> ~~Grows~~ terrifyingly simple
> Against our wretched times
> a
> Like hand~~s~~ within this station
> ~~When-along-its-endless-rhymes~~
> ~~Parting-begins-its-pull~~
> ~~With~~
>
> ~~explosion-of-departure~~
> Waiting the [???] mimes
> ~~Of-sorrow-and-this-pull~~
> Of ~~grief-that~~
> love, the   pull

The first two lines, though they were to be modified in the course of drafting, are in fact exactly as finally printed. The rhymes of the third stanza — "relation"/"station"; "times"/"mimes"; "simple"/"pull" — are all there too (though he was to try departing from them in his second draft). Yet the poem is incoherent concerning the image of the hand and its relation to the war in which he is involved. This takes in all some seven attempts at the third stanza to get right; though finally it gives one of the most memorable moments in Fuller's poetry. The central emotion is there from the beginning in the paradoxical phrase "terrifyingly simple". Bringing the hands of the second stanza into relation with that emotion so as to focus it (and doing this in the rhyme-scheme already laid down) was the problem of the poem — and its eventual triumph.

A fluent opening, followed by problems at the end may be the story of the writing of many poems. As Robert Frost explained in "The Figure a Poem Makes", he eventually had to face the problem that he had created for himself with the interlocking rhyming stanzas of "Stopping by Woods on a Snowy Evening": at the end of the poem, the poet has to get out of what he has got into and, at the same time, make it seem the inevitable conclusion, bringing together everything that he had started up earlier.

A poem whose drafting did not follow the usual Fuller pattern is "Essential Memory", written at about the same time as "Thirty Years On". The printed version begins:

Fourth of October 1973:
I pick the date to form a line of these
Iambics that keep falling in in threes.

This is more or less how the poem began in the notebook — Fuller writing down a date, "2nd October 1973", because it made "a line in these/Five-stressed iambics". He got no further than his third stanza before he stopped. The second draft (in which he removes the partial redundancy of "Five-stressed iambics") also gets hung up on the third stanza; and he goes back over this part of the poem five times before leaving it.

These attempts form the last entries in the notebook that ran from October 1971 to October 1973. Like "Thirty Years On", with which its drafting is interspersed, "Essential Memory" was continued in a similar notebook that covered what was evidently a very prolific period from October 1973 to November 1973. However, in contrast with "Thirty Years On", the drafting gives the sense that Fuller is looking for where to go in the poem. It is worked on initially down to the phrase "Essential memory", and then taken up again immediately after "Thirty Years On" had been returned to and completed. At the end of the final draft of that poem, Fuller has a note to himself: "Can we love retrospectively the dead/We never knew" — phrases that become part of "Essential Memory". Hardly applicable in one sense to the poem about his mother's Christmas gift, they nonetheless show how the two poems are linked in their preoccupation with our relation with the dead.

Coming back to "Essential Memory" after this, Fuller finds the nub of the poem in a passage concerning the death of Auden, which leads into the reflection, "Autumn: the leaf more insecurely hangs/Than hung the fruit", with which he stops. He then drafts the poem down to its conclusion; but, after a little tinkering, crosses out the last four stanzas and copies them as he wants them; only again, after some redrafting, to cross out the final stanza, and then revise it to give its final form. He then dates the poem as it stands with its many alterations: 16.x.73.

The date at the beginning of the poem seems clearly to have been the date on which it was begun; and the mere fact that the date formed an iambic line may have been the impulse to write the poem. One is left wondering whether he had any sense then that it would lead to a poem built round a recollection of the death of Auden. The groping progress would seem to suggest that he did not. Of course, the extent to which a poem is "there" when the poet starts the actual process of writing must in all cases be difficult to pin down. When does the process of writing begin ? To what extent do we know what we are going to say before we open our mouths and embark on saying it? In what way does thought exist prior to articulation? Poetry, after all, may be viewed as a highly complex form of articulation.

It is interesting to turn to a later poem that evidently also gave Fuller some trouble — one in which, in fact, he seems to be groping for the poem as he drafts it through nine pages of drafts. It is one of the "Mianserin Sonnets", so called because they were composed when he had been prescribed the drug Mianserin; and here the problems of composition are related to the more structured rhyming form of the poem.

This poem where, as in so much of his later work, he looks out on the garden of his home, begins as a brief jotting in which he attempts to capture the startling impression of the moon seen through the branches of a poplar:

> to see
> Amazing, the full November moon
> <u>familiar</u>
> ~~hattered-Broken-by-the-tall-poplar-so-usual-by-day--~~
> Shattered by the poplar that by day
> Is so ~~fam~~ innocuous
>
> Amazing, to see the full November moon
> Shattered by the poplar that by day
> Is so innocuous, although I soon   drink
> ?   (At evening time, quite far away
> (From sun-downer time find other startling things

At the next shot he gets the first three lines as they are to remain (except for the later substitution of "Astonished, I view" for the first three words):

> Amazing to see the full November moon
> Shattered by the poplar that by day
> Is so comparatively unromantic

The poem that is to flow from these lines is still to be found. However, he gets into it nicely in the next draft; which, after some reworking, he copies out "in clear" on the next page:

> Amazing to see the full November moon
> Shattered by the poplar that by day
> Is so comparatively unromantic.
> What phantoms may buttonhole me, let alone
> Invade imagination? Some nude fay
> Warmth underlying chill, in my gerontic

Pacings encountered. Yet one knows too well

         a

The tale must have / twist: the wolf succeeds

                 stone

In kidding the ~~little~~ kids but gets a / belly-ache

                 or one simply wakes

In olden times wishing was still worthwhile

~~As thus the Grimms~~

The Grimms remarked. My ancient times are new.

On the way "Some nude fay/Flesh damp & chill beside my garden" had been modified to remove the direct, erotic reference to "flesh"; while the irony of his own situation, modern and sceptical, but also aging himself, was brought out by substituting "in my gerontic/Pacings" for the reference to the garden. The first of these changes seems to have been made at once; but, from the pattern of handwriting, one has the sense that the drafting proceeded without the second new line being completed, until Fuller saw the possibility of a rhyme for "romantic" (difficult to find) in the word "gerontic".

Once he had got to this stage, everything from "What phantoms" to "Pacings" was to stay unchanged with the poem to the end (except for the introduction of "the" before "Imagination"); while the remark of the Brothers Grimm, after much rephrasing and rearrangement, was to provide the conclusion of the poem, and serves as a goal to which the rest of the writing is directed. The wolf and the children, from the world of the Brothers' Grimm, were also to remain with the poem, though their accommodation involved considerable work. Indeed, in the next draft he has three shots at the second half of the poem; and in the following draft, two. By that time the full rhyme scheme is firming up, something that seems to be indicated by ticks beside some of the later lines.

Some of the manoeuvring in these last lines is the product of the very tight economy of a sonnet of this kind, in which there is an exploration of feeling involving ironic changes of perspective: the story of the children and the wolf has to be reduced to a couple of lines, or else it will be too long for its role in the poem. All this has to be sandwiched, with much else, between the opening half, already written, and the remark of the Brothers Grimm that is to make the end.

In the next draft, Fuller finds an ironic point of contemporary contrast in the sound of the "News in the room behind". The sonnet emerges complete; and, after some tuning up, Fuller copies it out as the final version, dating it 25.xi.83. The conclusion reads:

> Yet of course I know
> How tales end in an unexpected blow,
> Oft for the old and ugly. The vulpine smile
> May kid the kids, but then a belly-ache
> Of stones does in the wolf. One must admit —
> News in the room behind, blazing the fake —
> The Brothers Grimm were right to limit it
> To olden times — that wishing was still worthwhile.

Yet Fuller was evidently dissatisfied. He copied out the poem in full again almost as it was, and then crossed out the last five lines. The awkward nexus after the dash in the last two lines evidently troubled him, as he went at these first. In addition, the word "fake", offering a slightly gratuitous and commonplace contrast of present and past, had evidently been arrived at as a rhyme for "belly-ache". Now "belly" suggests the much more effective and natural colloquialism "telly". This involved some further rearrangement, and led to a complete rewriting of the last eight lines, with the introduction of an additional new rhyme "more"/"yore", evidently in an attempt to make the conclusion flow more naturally.

He then must have copied the poem out in what he felt *was* a final version, with the title "Fairy Tales", the date 27.xi.83, and the annotation "Quite right". However, this version was also to be subject to considerable alteration, not all of which survives. Beside a version dated 28.xi.83 (and possibly thought to be final) there is a note "Revised on scrap — lost, alas." Seven pages on in the notebook, the poem is re-transcribed exactly as later printed. It is only in this version that the remark of the Brothers Grimm is made to flow naturally:

> In fact, I'm sure
> (News of great follies behind me on the telly)
> The Grimms were right, confining to days of yore
> The truth of the maxim 'wishing is still worthwhile'.

The sonnet is in syllabic verse, characteristic of Fuller's work in this period. The basic unit is an eleven syllable line, deviating by one syllable from the count of the iambic pentameter, and hence permitting effects similar to those of irregular iambic pentameter lines, while also encompassing the possibility of lines like "Is so comparatively unromantic", where any regular rhythm suggested by surrounding lines collapses. In the original "final" version of 25.xi.83, the conclusion, except for the final line, consists of ten-syllable lines. As Fuller remarked in his Oxford lectures: "Even numbers tend to the iambic";[1] and these lines may be scanned as iambic pentameter, with some reversals:

> ∪ – | ∪ – | ∪ – | ∪ – | ∪ –
> May kid the kids, but then the belly-ache
>
> ∪ – | ∪ – | ∪ – | ∪ – | ∪ –
> Of stones does in the wolf. One must admit—
>
> – ∪ | ∪ – | ∪ – | ∪ – | ∪ –
> News in the room behind, blazing the fake—
>
> ∪ – | ∪ – | ∪ – | ∪ – | ∪ –
> The Brothers Grimm were right to limit it
>
> ∪ – | ∪ – | ∪ – | ∪ ∪ – | ∪ –
> To olden times— that wishing was still worthwhile.

In the final printed version, only one of the last five lines ("Of stones will wipe it off. In fact, I'm sure") has ten syllables; there being only one other ten-syllable line in the whole poem. The final revision may in part have been prompted by the wish to subdue the iambic effect.

In any poem, several dimensions are being developed at any moment: imagery; figurative use of language; tone; irony; aural effects. The list is as long as the possibilities afforded by the use of language; and within these various categories of effect, sub-effects and tensions between effects may be developed. In some poems there are important continuities associated with the deployment of certain effects; while, with other effects (or in other poems) such continuities are not developed or utilised. In Dylan Thomas's "A Winter's Tale" there is a heavy orchestration of diction and imagery—words and images such as "cup", "bread", "snow", "vale"—that serves not only to tie the poem together, but to reinforce and partially carry its central emotional drive. In Fuller's poetry, it is clear that the main thrust of the poem is carried by explicit statement—by narrative, argument, reflection. Ironies within that pattern of explicit statement are importantly utilised; and variations of tone are essential to the emotional impact of the poems. These variations of tone—and much else in the poetry—are dependent upon the creation of a sense of voice and variation in that voice; and this, in turn, is dependent on diction and the associations that words have in everyday use. There is little orchestration of imagery and figurative language in Fuller's work;

and figurative language often appears in the ironic use of cliche. The rational surface of Fuller's poetry, frequently remarked upon, goes about the business that it seems to be going about, and is not qualified by undercurrents of less rational effects. Even the music does its most important work in sustaining the sense of a particular voice articulating the poetry.

The notebooks reinforce this analysis. We seldom encounter attempts to follow out a particular image, or a change of direction in a poem consequent on the abandonment of an image. Fuller concentrates on continuities of narrative, reflection and argument; and the supportive effects that are worked on in the drafting are ones of tone, diction, rhythm.

One thing that might be remarked upon is his devotion to traditional forms that might appear odd in a poet who seems to seek to develop a natural and unartificial surface for his poems. In some of the poems examined here — those that appeared in *From the Joke Shop* (1975) — rhyme is not used; and, in his later sonnet sequences, *Subsequent to Summer* (1985) and *Available for Dreams* (1989), Fuller largely avoids rhyme, using the ghost of the tight traditional form almost to suggest that experience is not to be imposed upon by such artificial constraints. (This was somewhat the effect produced by Robert Lowell's handling of the sonnet in *Notebooks* (1969).) Ian Hamilton once remarked of Fuller that "there is always [the] suspicion that he feels not only rhyme but all the taxing stanzaic patterns he sets himself to be 'useless', in the sense that they have no central expressive or synthesizing function in the modern world";[2] yet, in a contribution to a symposium in *Agenda*, Fuller spoke of the looser stress pattern of syllabic verse being "validated" by rhyme, and remarked that he could "hardly bear verse which has not got at least. . .the ghost of some metre lurking behind the arras".[3]

The problem is very central to any sense of the validity of poetry. After all, as Marianne Moore so famously remarked, "there are things that are important beyond all this fiddle" ("Poetry"); and, to the naive enquirer, saying things straight out without embellishment ought to be the clearest way of getting at the truth. One has the sense that Fuller had a grudging respect for that position; and that this, in fact, is the source of an important tension in his poetry.

This takes us back to an earlier observation — his fluency, and the way in which the drafting proceeds, in many cases, rapidly under the direction of narrative and reflection, to be "tuned up" later on. And this observation reinforces in turn our sense of the particular nature of Fuller's poetry and the qualities for which we value it. If we place Fuller's poetry beside that of Larkin (with which it shares a disposition to cultivate the rational and the colloquial), we see at once that Larkin, in poems such as "Church Going" (considered in its day such a deflative performance), is drawn to much grander resonances than Fuller would allow himself.

Indeed, the notebooks reveal that the mode of drafting is all of a piece with Fuller's attitude to poetry and with the type of poetry he sought to create. The effects that are dominant in his poetry are the effects on which he expended the most work.

NOTES

1. Fuller, R. *Owls and Artificers* (London: Deutsch, 1971) 54.
2. Hamilton, I. *A Poetry Chronicle* (London: Faber, 1973) 89.
3. Fuller, R. Contribution to "A Survey on Rhyme" *Agenda* 28,4 (Winter 1991) 16–17.

ALLAN AUSTIN

Roy Fuller's Fiction:
A Modest Proposal

I am sure my delight at the publication of *Stares* was typical of Roy
Fuller admirers. In a letter to me some years ago he expressed the
unlikelihood of another novel, and passing time seemed to confirm
this; but since energy and discipline had long characterized Roy Fuller
my initial surprise on learning of *Stares* soon gave way to knowing
inevitability. A visitation by the Muse of Fiction (to take a hint from
Fuller's last memoir, *Spanner and Pen*), after nearly twenty years is
cause for celebration in principle; in fact, this engaging, thoughtfully
touching, and solidly crafted book, among the author's best, merits
further hurrahs.

Rumination is the *sine qua non* of Fuller's poetry; confession, of his
fiction. In depicting the private institution for the disturbed, Stares,
where patients are encouraged to talk out their pasts, the author
provides himself with splendid confessional opportunities. William
Toyne, the Fullerian narrator, possessed of his own secrets, has the
natural facility of prompting, without deliberate effort, disclosure
from fellow inmates, the selflessness to register these, and the wit
to provide engaging commentary. Sardonically he characterizes himself as "the detached observer" whose "judicious mind and balanced
prose" dilutes "outrageous emotions."[1] The creative man of the cast,
Toyne, enlisting the aid of Chekhov, serves to validate again the worth
of the artist, and his work, in a troubled world; he also reminds us
that the artist, sharer of the quotidian, is not immune from personal anguish. Without, however, discounting Toyne's therapeutic
significance within Stares, the book's crucial drama is the narrator's
redemptive ascendance through language.

Turning from *Stares*, the question I ponder is the survival prospects
of Fuller's fiction. Undoubtedly it is quite right that this distinguished
man of letters should have considered himself equally poet and novelist; yet this view must be balanced by the critical perception of
him as fundamentally the former. Typically, the review of *Stares* in
The Times Literary Supplement closed with a reference to "Fuller's
more important work, his poetry."[2] In so far as these contempora-
neous literary stock market issues are assertible, Fuller's place in the
twentieth-century poetry canon is assured. One simply cannot say

the same for the fiction. In *Spanner and Pen*, Fuller, noting the poor sales of recent paperback reissues of two of his earlier novels, reported the publisher's decision to cancel the planned publication of two additional novels.[3] The problem with the security of Fuller's fiction, as I see it, is not with the novels *per se*, but with the *realpolitik* of the novel context.

Recent decades have witnessed a novel reader's paradise. Fiction thy name is abundance. England has never had so many accomplished practitioners writing simultaneously, though a principle involving the distribution of talent may be operative. Who, we may reasonably wonder, out of the myriads will survive, since that elusive literary category, the major novelist, appears unfilled to this observer. Consider listing the notable British novelists publishing during Fuller's lifetime. Would one stop with twenty names? Thirty? Forty? Confronted by such a listing, the casual reader might assume critical judgement to be in total abeyance. As well, of course, the novel flourishes elsewhere and not least in tides from the Third World. In any case, Fuller's mandarin stories, nominally confined to the clericy, are not aggressively competitive. At one point in his memoirs, in a tone I judge to combine wistfulness and hopefulness, Fuller remarked on the slow emergence of George Gissing as one of the elect company of survivors.[4]

It is pleasing to think that Fuller enjoyed much satisfaction in creating his fiction, and derived a reasonably enhancing fiscal reward. Perhaps he should have been content with this; perhaps, like many contemporary writers, he should have adopted a *Rubaiyat* outlook and let the future go; yet it is both insensitive and unimaginative not to recognize the writer's natural longing for posterity. In *My Child, My Sister*, Albert Shore thinks personal death does not carry as much terror for the writer as the thought of his work entering oblivion. He wonders if his novels will survive, and one in particular. (9) Here those of us who would foster Fuller's cause may find a useful hint. I would argue that at least one of Fuller's novels, *My Child, My Sister*, merits survival into the future. Hopefully the following revisitation can contribute to this book's inclusion in the century's chronicle of enduring novels.

My Child, My Sister is purportedly reminiscence. Though a successful novelist, Albert Shore expresses reservations about fiction: how it may substitute the gesture or the image for the truth; how it may be driven to distortions. He also covertly admits an inability to write hopeful fiction since the novelist is bound, so he believes, to be general and so record the still sad music of humanity. Hence this work where, recording the specifics of his own recent experience, a considerable measure of the positive is attainable. While involved in the events he now retrospectively records, he completed his latest novel, *Stephanie*, largely based on the life and death of the woman with whom he happily lived for many years. When the novel is finished, Shore thinks, "Suppose one's theme was renewal, optimism, life, the reverse of all" to be found in *Stephanie*. (134) *My Child, My Sister* is essentially the realization of this heady, seemingly uncharacteristic, impulse. Surprisingly, yet fortuitously, the most significant of Shore's unresolved past, as if it has merely been biding its time, resurfaces in a manner calculated to stroke a writer's aesthetic sensibility and resume its pattern.

The recording of events affords Shore the therapeutic consolation of a cleansing unburdening. Here he lays bare his innermost thoughts, fears, longings, perceived weaknesses, foibles, prejudices, limitations, and egoism: a portrait, in fact, touchingly human. Though the anxiety ever present at the cutting edge of existence is palpable on every page of a narrative recording the unceasing processes of loss and gain, the book is transcendent. Shore has cause to be anxious about much: Fabian's future, his political activities, and his involvement with Frances; the increasing signs of his own advancing years; the society changing — declining? — about him; his creative resources and artistic reputation; renewed contact with Eve and Christopher; Flip's emergent condition; and increasingly, and somehow embracing all else, distressing evidence of misreading.

The initial instances of misreading are innocent enough. The sound of the crying infant is found to have its origins in the human breast, and the startling mouse skull proves to be a decayed molar. These humorously foreshadow profounder blunders. That awareness after the fact must be accepted as one of life's inevitabilities does not lessen the dread of commitment. One might have anticipated the short-lived marriage of Shore — mid-thirties set-in-his ways academic bachelor — and the undergraduate Eve; but who could have foretold his intensely insistent fatherhood? How poignant Eve's departure coinciding with the baby bird's arrival as Shore registers the pathos of his, Fabian's, and the bird's situation. Compassion, as the book's title (from a poem by Baudelaire) hints, is the engine of Shore's life, though even his warmest impulses suffer self-inflicted ambiguities thrown off by his restless mind. Big of frame and big of heart, much of his conduct camouflages vulnerability.

Over the years Shore has fixed in his mind images of Eve and of Christopher and of their marriage, and of their probable feelings

toward himself. Even with the passage of time and the fulfilling relationship with Blanche these images have continued to trouble him
and to stir unworthy feelings of resentment and dislike. It is, then,
late in the book, with old relationships resuscitated, no small matter
for Shore to wonder at and indeed accept the wrongness of his imagination in these matters. Eve, frozen in time for him, has, naturally,
aged. In his flirtation with ignoble self-pity, Shore has denied feelings
on the other side. Eve tells him of Christopher's hurt over a presumed
portrait of himself in one of Shore's novels, and Christopher tells him
how long it took Eve to get over Shore's determined possession of
Fabian. As the characters of Eve and Christopher clarify for him,
as the shape of their lives emerges, Shore's sense of pathos is in the
ascent. The immediate issues of the Fabian-Frances relationship, and
of Flip's decline, both extend and compound this. In one alarming
moment, thinking of how he has in the past years instinctively wished
ill to Eve and Christopher, Shore startles himself with the possibility
that Flip's situation is this appalling realization.

   My Child, My Sister is a study in paradox. It is — or is it not? —
strange that the seeming catastrophe of Shore's personal life, Eve's
flight, is its true making, possibly crucial to the successful creative
one: the anomalous enhancing betrayal? Consider: it yielded the
rich relationship between father and son; it produced the chastened
post-Eve man whom Blanche loved; it led to the creation of Flip and
her eventual and crucial entry into Shore's life: it brought together
Fabian and Frances, from whose pairing flows the story of reunion,
recognition, recovery, and renewal culminating in the enchanting form
of Freda (and, by the by, what *is* the significance of the recurring
"f's" of Fabian, Frances, Flip and Freda? fate? family? forgive-
ness? future? fulfilment?) Humanistically bent, Shore gently but
determinedly drives home the basic lessons (forever needing reasser-
tion) about first impressions being uncertain, and experience calling
for openness and humbleness since retrospection so often holds significance. Shore's story echoes W.B.Yeats's oft asserted observation
about the difficulty of self-forgiveness; but by the close, warmed and
creatively stimulated by the little Freda, he knows peace. From out
of this flows the most telling matter of his writing career: his gift to
us.

   The dark side of what Freda represents is, of course, Flip. Like the
young bird with whom she is linked, Flip is another call of the crying baby. She is also mystery entering into the quotidian. Inevitably
the supremely rational Shore is drawn to her. His motives for pursuing their relationship, he intimates, are mixed, though the purity

of his love is not in doubt. The concupiscence is authentic enough:
as he notes, neither age nor particular relationships deter the voyeur.
Flip's proximity during their first drive together makes a strong vis-
ceral registration, companionship of a nubile female registering as a
rare treat; but Flip's troubling, enigmatic comments surely are the
true allure. Shore's wondering if his surreptitious pursuit of her is
calculated to disturb Eve and Christopher can be dismissed as fodder
drawn from a mind given to self-abnegation and fascinated by alter-
natives. Likewise, the hints that Flip's upbringing is at the root of
her identity problem, that her place in the family quartet accounts
for her sense of worthlessness, seem no more than a natural need
of the rational to defuse the inexplicable. Eve, in frustration, may
well ask why Flip's illness is happening to them. Life, obviously, is
more difficult (if not impossible) for some. Faced with the minor poet
James Blagden, Shore registers the guilt of the strong confronting the
weak. Alone among his fellow committee members, Shore is prepared
to risk giving the unpromising Blagden further funding, knowing the
others will judge him more the fool. Shore is uneasy about Fabian
demonstrating in the streets; but son is really emulating father.

Flip's art comes as a double surprise to Shore, with both subject
matter and unanticipated level of execution giving pause. As fellow artists they make their deepest contact, and the veteran Shore
is comfortable in proffering advice. Still, Flip's decline into institu-
tionalization is relentless. Early on Shore anticipates the process and
sees too, in his first visit to the private clinic, that her environment is
self-defeating, that "she will never get better here." (170) Shore sees
in Flip the daughter he might have had; Flip herself arrives at a sense
of the same relationship. Her tears at the close of their Tate Gallery
evening may register regret at what might have been. When the crisis
of the cigarette burn confronts them it is Shore who virtually assumes
command, though circumstances circumscribe what he can do. His
entry into Flip's life comes too late.

My Child, My Sister is enriched by Shore's inevitable preoccupation with the nature of the artist and his work. His asides provide
attractive glimpses into the workshop. He subscribes to the theory of
the artist being in some degree abnormal and creativity hence com-
pensatory. He makes clear that the writer is driven to produce by the
recurring need to prove himself again and again, an activity he links
with love. Shore's confessing extends to his professional position as
well. Supposed sage of life, he is repeatedly struck by what he has not
fathomed in "the complexity and potentiality" of personal relations.
(28) The modern canvases at the Tate disconcert him with a sense

of hardly belonging to his own epoch; but for him, the writer's work must necessarily be bound by the limitations of his own experience.

Shore's doubting is a strength of his wisdom. Life, he sees, for all its rich diversity of surface, is fundamentally thin, and the greatest lesson to learn — likely later than sooner — is reconciliation, the fact of death ultimately driving this home. Only latterly do we come to see that Shore has articulated for us problems with which his text has had to wrestle. The presentation of himself has involved the primary challenge of aiming for seriousness while eschewing "priggishness, mawkishness, solemnity, turgidity". (70) During the writing of *Stephanie* he discovers that his heroine's death is really not the end of the novel though this has been his working assumption. This is the kind of instinctive recognition that stirs the creative forces. Can Flip's doom have been envisioned as the end of this story? If so, life fortuitously determined otherwise. While judging Shore to have effectively resolved these matters, the critic will also note Shore's position *vis-à-vis* him. "How can a writer possibly reject a criticism based on meaning, a criticism devoted to finding out what is really meant?" (125) Several of his personal ticks are nicely registered. He is not particularly happy at being labelled "laureate of the domestic," and suggests the insufficiency of this. (79) He is piqued by the regard some of the younger novelists receive; since, from his viewpoint, they have merely done what he accomplished a decade earlier more elegantly.

Reconciliations cannot restore Flip, though Eve finds comfort in Shore's involvement and concern. What can be done for Flip will be done; nothing more is possible and to this one must be reconciled. The time lapse before the closing scene is proper and Shore is right to let Flip recede into the background. To the fore is the marriage of Fabian and Frances, the offspring Freda, and the trusty grandfather. Lucky Freda, already at some level conscious of life's imperfections since "bear is not very well to-day," and the recipient of enlightening insight from grandfather, "The little girl says: 'The trouble with you, Bear, is that you think you've got the monopoly of life and virtue, and the trouble with you, Snake, is that you can't help being a snake.'" (188) In Albert Shore, his story, and his meditations, Roy Fuller renders a memorable and valuable account, the richer we will be for retaining.

NOTES

All quotations from *My Child, My Sister* are from the edition of 1965 published in London by Andre Deutsch.

1. Fuller, R. *Stares* (London: Sinclair Stevenson, 1990) 78.
2. *Times Literary Supplement* Jan. 11, 1991, 17.
3. Fuller, R. *Spanner and Pen* (London: Sinclair Stevenson, 1991) 134.
4. *Spanner and Pen*, 145.

Barbara Gabriel

The Corpse in the Library:
Roy Fuller and the Literary Crime Novel

> It certainly seemed as though he might sleep... He set himself one of
> his usual anti-insomnia problems, not too easy, not too hard. Living
> English poets through the alphabet. Auden, American, perhaps. Al-
> lott, then. Barker. C was a little more difficult. Church. Durrell. E
> escaped him at first. Every was rather too recondite to be fair, but
> he certainly recalled a poem in the Criterion once . . . His thoughts
> drifted off. (*Crime Omnibus* 190)

When George Garner, in *The Second Curtain*, retires to his bed only
to find he cannot sleep, he counts poets rather than sheep, a surprisingly high-flown enterprise for the protagonist of a crime novel. Yet
no other form of literary production more completely confounds the
now suspect distinction between "high" and "low" culture than the
detective story and its near-relation, crime fiction. "Not only do intel-
lectuals read detective stories," Michael Holquist reminds us, "they
write them. It is significant that in such tales the body is usually
discovered in the *library*, for their authors tend to be oppressively
bookish".[1]

Roy Fuller's three crime novels, all written in the immediate post-
war period between 1948 and 1954 and collected, with the neat symmetry of a triptych, in *Crime Omnibus* (1988), are full of self-consciously literary moments, tracing the historical arc of crime fiction with
deliberate ironies. The first two novels in the volume, *With My Little
Eye* (1948) and *The Second Curtain* (1953), echo both Dickens and
the Victorian novelist's own mentor in the writing of *The Mystery
of Edwin Drood*, Wilkie Collins. The final story, *Fantasy and Fugue*
(1954), is even more deliberately a fiction in the shadow of Edgar
Allen Poe, undisputed father of the modern detective story. It is a
submerged drama of crime and guilt told by a Dostoevskian narrator as underground-man. These literary traces are, often, themselves,
false clues, operating in a narrative structure whose very function is
simultaneously to advance and forestall its own resolution. As Dennis
Porter tells us, the state of more or less pleasurable tension surrounding the crime story's unravelling *depends* on "something not happening too fast".[2] The detective fiction's formula, in other words, offers a

strikingly clear example of the general narrative principle which Russian formalist Victor Erlich has called "deliberately impeded form".[3]

In the case of Fuller's crime novels, the reader-as-literary-sleuth comes up short in a number of instances. Sir Walter Scott's *The Black Dwarf* provides key evidence for the adolescent detective of *With My Little Eye* and Poe's *The House of Usher* frames the family romance of *Fantasy and Fugue*, turning up important clues to the murder mystery in the process. On the other hand, the reader who understands the relevance of George Garner's persistent reading of Dickens's *Our Mutual Friend* (where the drowned man surfaces at the end) to *The Second Curtain* is destined to get it all wrong and be punished for literary *hubris*.

Yet Fuller's often ironic use of literary motifs throughout these novels is structurally rooted in conventions of novelistic perspective. In the Introduction to *Crime Omnibus*, he acknowledges "that the three novels raise the Jamesian question of the narrating consciousness, always acute in the conscientious crime novel" (*Crime Omnibus* 9). He also confesses to a "passion" for Collins in the period and it could be argued that his own close linking of character and mode of seeing even more directly echoes the author of *The Woman in White* and *The Moonstone*. Detective fiction has often been described as the very model of reading as hermeneutical exercise. It is also one which foregrounds what Bakhtin has called the dialogical relationship of subject and object in any production of meaning, a connection Collins had earlier explored in the pioneering point-of-view experiments of *The Woman in White*. In that novel, Collins dramatizes the way in which professional habits of mind, among other things, shape a whole way of knowing. It is an insight Fuller repeats comically in *With My Little Eye*, where the presiding magistrate, and father of the narrator, is preoccupied with summing up the legal niceties of his judgment even after the complainant has been shot dead in the courtroom before his eyes.

What Fuller's crime novels have in common, then, are protagonists who are, themselves, men of letters, refracting all of life through a literary lens. For the first two central characters, at least, the terms and images of both their waking hours and their dreams are coaxed into shape by what they have *read*, private existence experienced only at a safe remove. It takes a murder, a small crack in the moral firmament, to challenge their habitual responses.

George Garner of *The Second Curtain* is a penurious publisher's reader and would-be biographer of the young Alexander Pope; Harry Sinton of *Fantasy and Fugue* is the broken scion of a publishing house.

The only variation in these stories serves to confirm the rule: Frederick French, the youthful narrator of *With My Little Eye* is a bookish schoolboy with more experience of literature than life. By his own admission, "the way he writes — the very fact that he troubles to write at all — proclaims him to be a precocious highbrow" (*Crime Omnibus* 14).

With My Little Eye has been described by Julian Symons as "a perfect example of a modern crime story",[4] its deserved status all the more surprising for its publishing history. It appeared in the wake of Fuller's adventure story for children, *Savage Gold* (1946), published by John Lehmann Limited. The children's story was one of the first publications of the new firm established by Lehmann, following his departure from Hogarth Press. In a post-war period in which there was a shortage of books, it quickly sold out its printing of ten thousand copies. Having established the strength of the market for juvenile writing, it encouraged the publication of *With My Little Eye* with the sub-title, "A Mystery Story for Teenagers". In spite of its adolescent narrator, several reviewers felt that the book might have been brought out as an ordinary crime novel. In retrospect, they were right, not just because of the subtlety of language and characterization, but because the ironic filter of the narrative was clearly designed for an adult audience that could recognize its disjunctions. Like all of the novels in the volume, it explores the detective fiction's traditional twinning of meaning and morals, a connection the precocious protagonist fully understands. The "hunt for a murderer — fictional or in real life," he tells his father, "satisfies a moral longing":

> It is all a part of the revolution of our time. We — my generation — have no general and dogmatic views about right and wrong. And yet we want good to be rewarded and evil punished. Murder is a happening which is quite unarguably evil even from our disillusioned viewpoint. And so in that little limited sphere we have a disproportionate interest. On a lower level, of course, the pursuit of a murderer has the interest of a puzzle. But if you go on to ask me why men are fascinated by puzzles, I am afraid I cannot answer you. (*Crime Omnibus* 70)

Julian Symons reminds us that the Second World War was a watershed in the history of the crime story. Not only did it challenge the rationality of crime fiction with its clockwork solution, but it put into question the Great Detective himself who "in a symbolic sense had failed to prevent the War".[5] What's more, the technology that had produced the images of the death camps had also, in another sense, made them possible. The innocent young protagonist of *With*

My Little Eye seems to understand this intuitively when he images
the crime in terms of a machine which, slowly but inexorably, comes
to take over a whole house.

But a new kind of puzzle paradigm was also gaining intellectual
ground, one which has traditional links with the crime novel. Freud
had read Dorothy Sayers as well as *Oedipus Rex*; his psychoanalytic
method itself proposed a spiralling movement backward to the hidden scene of the original and secret wound. Fuller's three crime novels
dramatically expose this historic relationship between Freud and the
detective story. They also invariably have a psychoanalytic knot.
The murdered man's sister in *The Second Curtain* reminds us of the
peculiar logic connecting murder and the unconscious. "Of course,"
says Miss Widgery, "there is a large part of everybody's life which
remains for the most part underneath the surface, which only shows
itself during a great disturbance" (*Crime Omnibus* 179). The "great
disturbance" which confronts Frederick French starts out with the
crime novel's mandatory corpse. Greater ripples still disturb the calm
surface of his life when he comes face to face, for the first time, with
the simultaneous attraction and danger of woman and his own bur-
geoning sexuality. It is a narrative movement of dark *bildungsroman*,
hidden beneath a largely comic-grotesque surface.

The story unfolds when the narrator, whose father is a county court
judge, attends a session in the decayed Victorian suburb of Heath-
stead to witness a routine case in which the owner of a house has
made application for repossession from a tenant. The landlord-owner
is shot dead in a courtroom scene reduced to a cinematic blur, in
which noone has seen the murderer, though French himself observes
a hunchback scurrying from the chamber. Inspector Toller appears on
the scene as a Dickensian comic figure who, like his ancestor Inspector
Bucket of *Bleak House*, the first detective in British fiction, relishes
eating while in hot pursuit of murder and its motives. Against this
detective of officialdom, the young narrator charts his own course as
rank amateur, but he is already quick to draw up a mental list of suspects in the Preece murder-mystery. Besides Savage, the tenant, all
too visible in the courtroom drama, there is that matter of the dwarf
and the previous complainant, Kekewich, whom Fuller himself modelled physically on J.D. Bernal, the Marxist scientist whom he met at
left-wing intellectual meetings after the war (*Crime Omnibus* 9). For
the young protagonist of the novel, the name of Kekewich is just a
sound, one which, when he learns a Christian name, inexplicably fills
the blank page with "two more sinister syllables" (*Crime Omnibus*
32). It is an entirely arbitrary signifier, driven only by the intensity

of his imagination. His is a life undiluted by experience, his intellect at this point almost exclusively language-bound. As throughout the narrative, it is his reading which provides him with his shaping clues. Adopting the persona of Hawkshaw the detective, he follows Kekewich to the races where he bets half a crown on a horse called "Murder Most Foul", his thirst raging "like the Ancient Mariner's" (*Crime Omnibus* 45). But it is another schoolboy text, this time his holiday reading, Sir Walter Scott's *The Black Dwarf*, which leads him to the identity of Elshie, the grotesque dwarf who will, himself, turn out to have a literary calling. As a captive in the hands of the Quilp-like figure, Frederick is abruptly wrested from the world of schoolboy innocence in more ways than one: "Throw away all that Matthew Arnold stuff, boy," he is told. "Poetry has been liberated since his day" (*Crime Omnibus* 106).

What follows is a send-up of the contemporary British poetry scene in which the dwarf recites poetry which echoes Dylan Thomas and sings the praises of *The New Revelation* anthology whose model is the ground-breaking *The New Apocalypse* (1939) anthology, edited by J.F. Hendry and Henry Treece. In *The Poetry of the Forties*, A.T. Tolley reminds us that the Apocalypse movement has been seen as summing up the "new romanticism" of the forties, identifying the decade in a general way.[6] In *The Second Curtain*, it surfaces as broad parody, located in a stylistically diverse narrative which involves, by turns, a visit to a spiritualist seance, a bearded woman, and a meeting with Mrs. Preece, who turns out to be a bigamist and fair-ground artist who could shoot a cigar out of her previous partner-husband's mouth, a talent which promptly adds her name to the list of suspects.

But Frederick French's most dramatic encounter is with the young daughter of the defendant in the court case which ended so abruptly in murder. Her "pointed lemur face" and ears, her hairy arms, and her erotically-charged nickname "Pussy" all hint at the liminal space between human and animal that she occupies in the protagonist's imagination.[7] She is a Keatsian type of *la belle dame sans merci*, drawn in the iconographic convention of Mario Praz's *The Romantic Agony*, a book George Garner takes down from the bookseller's shelf in *The Second Curtain* (*Crime Omnibus* 259). The story which she tells Frederick is an inset gothic tale, pitting a handsome young secretary, Mr. Brilliant, against his employer, the hideously deformed Dr. D'Eath, whom her father has forced her to marry.

In the end, it is Rhoda Savage who emerges as the fundamental puzzle of the text. If, in literary and pictorial convention, she is drawn in terms of the romantic decadence, she also recalls the cinematic heroines of *film noir* that popularized the detective genre for audiences of the nineteen-forties, following closely on the heels of Alfred Hitchcock's suspense masterpieces of the previous decade. Fuller's own comments on this cinematic borrowing provide a useful gloss:

> My reading of adult literature started in the high noon of the 'detective story', but by the time I came to attempt fiction myself the purely puzzle novel had been deepened and extended by several fine talents, perhaps most noticeably Greene and Eric Ambler. One must also add the name of Alfred Hitchcock, whose films of the 1930's often contained that potent ingredient — the sinister in banal settings. *With My Little Eye* in particular owes much to what might be called the nun in high heels or gun in the chapel's collecting-box syndrome. (*Crime Omnibus* 10)

Rhoda Savage's role in the narratives confirms Woman as the submerged mystery of the text in the Hollywood tradition which runs from Hitchcock to 'forties' dark film, whose most famous scripts, like Dashiell Hammett's *The Maltese Falcon* and Raymond Chandler's *The Big Sleep*, were themselves derived from classics in the nineteen-thirties school of American hard-boiled detective fiction. When Frederick first sees her, she is constructed as a filmic image, "[l]eaning against the post of the side gate. . .with a cigarette between her lips" (*Crime Omnibus* 79). The iconography fixes her as the seductive good-bad girl of *noir* caught in the moral chiaroscuro which defines itself first as crime and then as something more mysteriously bound up with sexuality itself. Soon enough, the young protagonist has an entirely new set of preoccupations. "I thought of Rhoda Savage. I never once thought of the Preece murder case" (*Crime Omnibus* 102).

The story returns, at the close, to its schoolboy frame, with the errant student chastised for the "frightful paper" he has handed in on *The Black Dwarf*. Forced to recount his adventures, he learns that his schoolmaster is, himself, "a rabid film fan", a taste he shares with his aged mother: "Always we seem to see an American murder mystery, where the murderer turns out to be a person of dubious identity, whose face has been seen throughout the film in the shadows, and whose strenuous activities have been, to me at least, of a disconcerting ambiguity" (*Crime Omnibus* 151).

It is a comic closing interlude, muted by the passage from innocence to experience that sums up the more sombre trajectory of the young French's adventure: "Henceforth I should always be this split person, and what was usually regarded as normal life — the Mr. Waggons and the Ronnie Reeveses — present itself. . .only as an interlude in the abnormal, the truly normal life of love and death" (*Crime Omnibus* 154).

The protagonist of the second story in the volume, *Second Curtain*, continues Fuller's tradition of the literary sleuth. Even more to the point, George Garner is an authority on crime fiction, lecturing at the Centre of Contemporary Culture on the social and historical shifts that produce the criminal as hero in novelists from Godwin and Bulwer-Lytton to contemporaries like Graham Greene. By profession, he is a publisher's reader and would-be biographer of the young Alexander Pope, but his own poetics are less neo-classic than romantic, an allegiance that mocks his own buried life.

The story opens with Garner's encounter with the poet and anthologist Fox, who has come to offer him the editorship of a literary quarterly to be funded by a wealthy captain of industry. Garner's heightened self-consciousness suggests the model of Joyce's adult Dubliners; he suffers the same atrophy of the heart as the central figure in "A Painful Case", the calculated order of his lodgings refusing the chaos of human connections. When he thinks of the wife who has left him he contemplates "a character out of a book, someone with clear edges, but without emotional tone" (*Crime Omnibus* 190). His most intense memories are frozen in late adolescence, marked by the ritual regularity of letter-writing to William Widgery, one of his closest school-boy friends. Into this tidy world comes the shock of a murder, the bloated corpse in the water none other than the very friend to whom he confided his recent good fortune.

Yet, as in *With My Little Eye*, it becomes increasingly clear that the narrative's mystery owes as much to the post-thirties fascination with depth psychology as to the leaner plot line of an unexplained corpse. In an ironic self-mirroring of the outer narrative, Garner, himself, is something of an amateur analyst. He determines that the guilt he feels about the lingering horror of war "must have an earlier origin than 1939. Since he believed quite implicitly in Freudian motivation he racked his memory. . .for an infantile clue to his present excessive emotion" (*Crime Omnibus* 162). He will wonder, in an Audenesque vein, why the spinsterish Viola Widgery never married, "what obstruction existed in her psyche" (*Crime Omnibus* 235) and accuse the attractive Sarah Freeman of "a conflict inside you that you haven't told me about or that you're ignorant of. Almost certainly a sexual conflict" (*Crime Omnibus* 218). But it is Sarah who has the final turn in their psychoanalytic *pas de deux*: "The trouble with you," she tells him pointedly, "is you've never lived" (*Crime Omnibus* 256).

Yet Garner's refusal of personal relations is intimately linked to the novel's dramatized debate around a literary poetics. Fox reminds his friend that the new periodical will be "[n]on-political, of course" (*Crime Omnibus* 161), a definition Garner challenges without understanding its full implications. His own agenda mirrors the Romantic revival of the nineteen-forties which dramatically supplanted the left-wing literary stance of an earlier decade. Garner's position, however, remains troubling, his ideal of the visionary imagination insufficient to carry the weight of recent history. Composing the opening Editorial in his head, he begins:

> the central fact of our time is Horror. . .The fantasy of the mature Romantics — of Poe, of Beddoes, of Hood — is our reality. *Their* reality distorted their dreams because it repressed their desires. *Our* reality can give us their dreams because our desires are independent of it. The lesson of the death camps is this: That man's spirit. . .(*Crime Omnibus* 162)

The elegiac tone strikes a false note as the degree zero of Auschwitz stops him dead in his tracks; and, indeed, in a series of reversals the novel emerges as a moral fable for the whole post-war literary scene. When the murderer turns out to be none other than the wealthy benefactor who has fingered him for the plum job only to silence him, Garner begins to see the magazine as something "like the Corporations of Fascism. . . " (*Crime Omnibus* 289). Suddenly the politics and poetics of non-engagement have a more sinister face, the manifesto of the untrammelled imagination the creed of the amoral criminal. In a condensed Existential twist at the close, the narrator discovers that he must choose, after all, repeating the word "responsibility", which echoes throughout the opening. The Fascist threat, so alive to the literary imagination of the nineteen-thirties, is not merely, Fuller's novel suggests, a bogeyman of the past. Murder here has a moral — and it is an urgent one for a generation still fresh from the wounds of war.

For Garner himself, the plot's unravelling offers only a partial education, though it is clear Fuller means him to stand in for a whole shift in the wind in British letters.[8] "We disillusioned denizens of the thirties," he muses ironically at the beginning of the novel, "are certainly the ones best fitted to play the stock markets of the forties" (*Crime Omnibus* 192). He rejects the offer of the Editor's post, then retreats out of cowardice both from charging the murderer and continuing his connection with his dead friend's sister. Once more, he is glad to "cast off for ever the intolerable burden of responsibility and duty" (*Crime Omnibus* 289).

As in *With My Little Eye*, the crime is imaged in the idiom of the machine, in that romantic dialectic of the organic and the mechanical which extends from Carlyle to D.H. Lawrence: "The alien machine into which he had accidentally dropped from his own harmless world had thrown him out again, broken, with scarcely any damage or interruption to its purposive wheels" (*Crime Omnibus* 290). The novel closes with a flashback to a scene of origins, as the young George recalls a frozen moment after the death of his mother, with his father weeping in a chair before the child of eight: "You're all I've got now, Georgie" (*Crime Omnibus* 290).

The subtle twinning of psychoanalysis and the detective story might have escaped many readers of Fuller's first two crime novels, but neither Julian Symons nor Fuller himself overlook the explicit Freudianism of *Fantasy and Fugue*. In the introduction to *Crime Omnibus*, the author refers the reader to *The Interpretation of Dreams* (1900). He might have just as appropriately directed them to Poe, who comes out of the same Symbolist twilight.

With its interior drama of unstable identity and its first person narrative, *Fantasy and Fugue* represents a distinct departure from the first two narratives. Yet its heightened Expressionist surface merely stylizes tensions and ambiguities already inherent in the first two murder mysteries, reminding us that the manifest crime of these narratives uncovers another scene of guilt or complicity. The logic is reversed in *Fantasy and Fugue*, where the narrator's perception of himself as murderer comes unstuck in the end, but something of the same tension between life and the closed world of the book persists: "All that was lacking was my own participation in this life — a life that had once been mine but which I somehow left behind: the elaborate but unfinished chapters a novelist finds in a forgotten drawer" (*Crime Omnibus* 294).

As the narrative opens, Harry Sinton contemplates the face of the stranger in the mirror before him, in a scene which, like the homoerotic choreography of the ending, echoes Wilde's *Dorian Grey*, and establishes the motif of the *doppelgänger*. Sinton's memory is a black hole stretching back at least three months to the time of his father's death. He reads an obituary of the poet and novelist, Max Callis, and concludes by some inexplicable act of logic that he has murdered him. The amnesiac murder plot recalls *Edwin Drood*, for the second time in the volume, but also Stevenson: "I could, like Hyde, have come and gone on errands that my Jekyll-self knew nothing about" (*Crime*

Omnibus 302). Pressed to find a motive, he self-consciously reconstructs his voyeuristic attraction to Fay Lavington, the dead man's mistress. As in both previous novels, woman is textually constructed by the protagonist as a mysterious Other, this time, a "weak, fragile, fluttering creature". In fact, she calls for the police and proves herself to be nothing of the sort, but her own ambiguity mirrors the shifting subjectivity of the narrator, who persistently images himself as duplicitous, "the furious character that hid itself behind the innocent exterior of the young highbrow publisher with a good war record, the member of the Sheridan, the flannel suit of clerical grey" (*Crime Omnibus* 320).

What releases Sinton's memory of a guilty failure to save a drowning friend is a theatrical adaptation of *The Possessed*. Dostoevsky's tortured protagonist focuses Rimmer's own nightmare world and, like the allusions to Poe's *The House of Usher*, it also self-consciously foregrounds the narrative's literary ancestors. What's more, as in the first novel and more ambiguously in the second, there are sexual knots in this drama.

The narrator's initial perception of himself as double turns on the contrast between the "so-called healthy life" of his sporting activities and the bookish world of Kafka, Hölderlin, and Proust, traces, he fears, of "l'homme moyen sensuel" (*Crime Omnibus* 294). It is a Decadent note which has a special meaning for a character whose own brother edits a periodical summed up as "*The Yellow Book* and bile" (*Crime Omnibus* 387). Harry Sinton's Oedipal drama, in short, quickly betrays itself as a crisis of sexual identity, his guilt inseparable from the interiorized image of the "stern" father at war with the "mother who had transmitted to me the evasive, cowardly, too sensitive veins of my character" (*Crime Omnibus* 395). His father's death, in turn, is feared as "a signal for me to lapse into an almost feminine state of remoteness from affairs. . . " (*Crime Omnibus* 396). The precise nature of this threat becomes clear when Harry Sinton encounters his "bachelor" brother's dissolute lover, who threatens him with the "faint perfumed odour of his sweat", his loud breathing as dangerous as "an erotic embrace" (*Crime Omnibus* 424). This is the real mystery at the heart of the protagonist's nameless guilt and it remains sufficiently hidden in the narrative as to constitute a surplus as much as a solution in the text, a literary puzzle, but also a lesson in what Eve Sedgewick terms the "epistemology of the closet".[9]

When the murderer turns out to be Sinton's homosexual brother, the unspoken double of the tale, it offers a new twist to George Garner's lecture on the historically sliding definitions of the hero and the criminal in the detective novel. Foucault reminds us that the very term "homosexual" is a nineteenth-century invention, taking its place in a proliferation of medical discourses around sexuality which required one to "*detect* it — as a lesion, a dysfunction, or a symptom. . . " (my italics).[10] Insofar as it destabilizes the precarious binary of sexual difference in the dominant culture, homosexuality always operates as a sign crime. It is, therefore, not surprising that in the immediate post-war period of the 1950's, when gender roles were being reified in a markedly conservative way, the homosexual should emerge in Fuller's text as the new type of the social criminal.

NOTES

Unless otherwise indicated, all quotations are from *Crime Omnibus* by Roy Fuller (Manchester: Carcanet, 1980).

1. Holquist, M. "A Whodunnit and Other Questions: Metaphysical Detective Stories in Postwar Fiction" in *The Poetics of Murder: Detective Fiction and Literary Theory* ed. G.W. Most and W.W. Stowe (London: Harcourt Brace Jovanovich, 1983) 149–174.
2. Porter, D. "Backward Construction and the Art of Suspense" in *The Poetics of Murder*, 327–340.
3. See *The Poetics of Murder* 329.
4. Symons, J. *Bloody Murder* (New York: Viking, 1984) 177.
5. *Bloody Murder*, 138.
6. Tolley, A.T. *The Poetry of the Forties* (Manchester: Manchester University Press, 1985) 101.
7. Dijkstra, B. *Idols of Perversity: Fantasies of Feminine Evil in Fin de Siècle Culture* (Oxford: Oxford University Press, 1986) 325.
8. *The Poetry of the Forties*, 9.
9. Sedgewick, E.K. *The Epistemology of the Closet* (Princeton: Princeton University Press, 1990).
10. Foucault, M. *The History of Sexuality* Vol. I (London: Allen Lane, 1979) 44.

PETER LEVI

The Oxford Lectures

When I was twenty, Roy Fuller was forty. He was always a poet I admired almost to idolatry, though he was too quizzical and just likeable to be wholly idolized, and he was sternly his own man, so that it has taken many years and several autobiographical writings for me to begin to understand him in the way that one soon (in retrospect it seems immediately) understood other poets in terms of who they were, what they believed, what were their social origins. He was swept into position as Professor of Poetry at Oxford in 1968 with a convincing list of supporters who were poets: I can remember no one who refused. They included Auden, Day Lewis, Larkin, Amis and Wain. As a Professor, he was honest and thoughtful and we all admired him. He was not as obvious a choice as he looked to us as young men, but he was serious, and the serious vote got him in.

In 1971 he produced his lectures in print as *Owls and Artificers*; and in 1973, the last ones as *Professors and Gods*. He turned out to be a brilliant lecturer with a strong technical theme for discussion. The grown-up academic world must have come as a surprise to him, as indeed in the mid-sixties it did to me, but it is only now that I see the importance of his having been an autodidact. Maybe most poets are that, in terms of poetry; but having found one's way, and being still struggling to find it, are essential qualifications for a professor of poetry. Robert Graves had been a bit too clever and paradoxical, like an intellectual conjurer; of course, he was a brilliant and famous poet, even an historical figure, but the questions or problems that interested us hardly engaged him any more. Roy Fuller took by comparison a severe line, which was mightily refreshing. A few passages in the second collection of lectures derived from literary journalism, and if he was like any existing kind of teacher or writer, it would be fair to say his lectures had a faint touch of *TLS* or *Southern Review* about them: yet they were livelier than any such journals are today, and also denser, like escapes in time from *The Criterion*, or even *Scrutiny*.

He began his five-year term as Professor with "Philistines and Jacobins", a revival of Matthew Arnold's topics in Arnold's farewell to Oxford as Professor about a hundred years before. Indeed, he handled those subjects with such masterly ease and depth that for the time

being he finally did exhaust them: at least that was what it felt like,
when I came to consider, as his successor in 1984, whether anything
should be said about Arnold. Roy Fuller's attack on the matter is
subtle and multiple as well as strong. "What are revolutions for,"
he innocently asks, "if not to increase the amount of sweetness and
light?" (*Owls and Artificers* 19) He expresses the view that it is only
"the absence of pretence, of duplicity, of fudging" (*Owls and Artificers* 22) in poetry, and not the poet's ideas or his jewel-like phrases,
that propound to us a notion of beauty and human perfection.

"In the disgust of a Swift or the malice of a Pope, the accidie of
an Eliot or the pride of a Yeats" (*Owls and Artificers* 22), it is the
genuineness that we should seek. There is a lot to be said for his
opinion, which I notice is in a special way true of his own poetry, and
of himself as a poet. He is perfectly genuine as well as mysteriously
gifted. As a thinker, he is in the tradition of Arnold at that writer's
best.

Technically, he is up to his neck in what to readers who are not
poets will appear confounding detail: the row he stirred up about
Pound's self-doubts is indigestible enough, but easily settled; it is
his favoured subjects like the verse technique of Daryush and Marianne Moore that are demanding. Thinking back, I do not believe we
thought them courageous, because we were prepared and we expected
to be puzzled as well as illuminated; yet I almost doubt whether a contemporary Oxford student audience would know what he was talking
about. The readership of a book after all is wider than the floating
population of a lecture hall. But one is constantly wrong in such
assessments; and, certainly in the sixties, I believed that I profited
greatly from these technical lectures, as well as from the discussion
that surrounded them. And in the preponderant treatment of such
great writers as Blake and Wallace Stevens, he is supreme. It may
be worth noting, by the way, that Blake is one of the oldest authors
he treats, though he does of course mention Pope and Shakespeare; I
also think it is true that Stevens, whom Americans think now is the
greatest modern poet, had less reputation twenty or thirty years ago.

Roy Fuller's titles were always enigmatic. "The Radical Skinhead"
was about Leavis-and-Snow highbrow and middlebrow culture; and
in that lecture he remarked "I don't seem to find among the young
now sufficient literary discrimination" (*Professors and Gods* 15). He
plunged deeply into a special kind of learning about *The Calendar of
Modern Letters*, the *New Left Review*, and "that ineffable writer of
letters to the press, G. Richards of Poole" (*Professors and Gods* 10).
If he quoted Thomas Mann, it was with the familiar seriousness of

a modern man, a reader of the more serious journals (as they then were); it did not sound like naming an academic figure. The first lecture of the second book was a blast of fresh air delivered with mastery. You might have thought that Leavis and Snow were old hat, since their controversy had occurred ten years before, but in his hands they opened up a subject which was morally fresh.

"The Osmotic Sap" led from Leavis on Shelley to attempts at scientific language in poetry; Auden scarcely shone, but the Professor, who was well entrenched by now, had a kind thought for Edgell Rickword, and took a full and revealing look at Tennyson as well as I. A. Richards. When he turned aside to make a pattern or to cut a dash like an ice-skater, he did so with conviction. "Every poet who has read James D. Watson's brilliant book, *The Double Helix*, must have been struck by the parallels between the discovery of the structure of the DNA molecule and the composition of a poem. . . " (*Professors and Gods* 39). Or we pondered on the discovery of satellites of Mars in 1877, which made Tennyson alter "the snowy poles of moonless Mars" to "the snowy poles and Moons of Mars", and the more recent observation that he should have said "snowless poles" (*Professors and Gods* 42). These small mineral pieces of information do for a lecture on poetry what historical anecdotes do for a historian; Roy Fuller a little shyly or gruffly offers us a fine selection of them. They are the fruit of an intelligent man constantly thinking about poetry. The bigger guns of this lecture, in which he engages Steiner in the *Cambridge Review*, are really only another fruit of the same process.

In the lecture that follows he moves easily from Aldous Huxley to Christopher Caudwell, Brecht, Pope's Homer and Auden. Reading it now one feels it is part of a culture to which one once strove to belong and which no longer exists: it was more left, more thorough, more unforgivingly severe, simply more serious than ours. The difference may be one of age rather than rage. After all, Roy Fuller always appeared perfectly friendly and never lost his temper, even about those he must have viewed as insects. Scorn was the worst he expressed, and that seldom: his strongest criticisms were massive silences. I do not think that there is any doubt that he relished the element of game that there is in poetry. It is known that his reading habits among old poets were conservative and probing, but he took his brief in these lectures to be the position of the modern poet. So when he dealt with confessional poetry, he did so in the light of Henry James, not without a glance towards Browning, and one of his brief but major encounters was with Nietzsche. He is always bookish, thank heaven, and I see now references I had forgotten — to Yeats and his notebooks, to

Benda's *Belphegor*, to Leavis on Montale. He will not let the modern classics rest on their shelf. He is like a dog who has cornered Leavis, Eliot and the rest, and will not let them go until they give a full account of themselves. This made him a wonderful teacher.

His "Poetry of the Two World Wars" has now become more or less the orthodox view, and his "Poetic Memories of the Thirties" are no longer surprising, though he makes a better case for Caudwell than most critics do. Here I must be autobiographical: I had read only some criticism by Caudwell, which I found in Bodley and enjoyed because it was full of fireworks; but in 1963, just out of curiosity, I took a Russian ship from Athens to Genoa. It was an awful occasion, and I ran away at Naples; but meantime I had discovered and read some of Caudwell's works, and the whole of John Cornford's poetry as well, in the ship's library. To my generation they were as writers wholly unknown, but ever since then I have carried a half-hearted banner for both of them.

> Some few in garrets starved or blue gulfs drowned
> Are lucky ones. . .

There is far more to be said for Roy Fuller as a critic than for Cornford as a poet: but the thought of these lines gives one pause, and I like the word "blue". What the entire lecture does is to make one think oneself back into the thirties, which it encompasses with an eery precision. In the last lecture in *Professors and Gods*, he gleefully lets loose his artillery for a few paragraphs against academic criticism, but he soon turns it on poets, that is on the greatest modern poets, and it is devastating. The lectures were always invigorating and the books are still inspiring. They will go on being read.

And after all, in spite of any doubts I have expressed, it is ridiculous to think that level, triumphant discourse has vanished: Roy Fuller's culture is alive and available while Mrs. Thatcher's is already growing misty. Roy Fuller's mental world is in a deep sense historical; one can feel backwards through it as well as fumble forwards. They used to say that by sixty one had the face one deserved; one certainly gets the mental and poetic culture one deserves. (In my own case I am surprised to discover it is heterogeneous, heterodox and heterosexual.) Roy Fuller's remained wonderfully varied and coherent, and never ceased to produce the most excellent poems. There is no decade indeed in which he did not produce better poems than before. In spite of his restraint, his underlying poetic culture is revealed, I believe, in these two books of lectures, to which I have had recourse more often than to anyone else's, even Auden's, and have always been fascinated.

NOTE

Unless otherwise indicated, quotations are from *Owls and Artificers* by Roy Fuller (London: Deutsch, 1971) and *Professors and Gods* by Roy Fuller (London: Deutsch, 1973).

George Woodcock

The Habit and the Habitat

I first encountered Roy Fuller in 1938. It was, in a small way, an
annus mirabilis for me, for two of my poems had been accepted by
Geoffrey Grigson for *New Verse*, and almost immediately afterwards
Julian Symons took three or four for *Twentieth Century Verse*. I
knew, at that time, very few people in the literary world, though I
had met some minor writers hanging around in Charlie Lahr's famous
Blue Moon Bookshop in Red Lion Street; and it was also in 1938 that
Lahr published my first collection, a modest foldover broadsheet entitled *Six Poems*. But I had already encountered Kathleen Raine and
Charles Madge, then her husband, who were running Mass Observation, that pioneer polling organization with its radical and literary
undertones; one was encouraged, among other things, to prepare the
reportage so favoured in the thirties (a day in an anonymous life —
that sort of thing). It was Charles and Kathleen who showed me in
their great rambling Blackheath house the issue of *New Verse* with
my poems; Grigson was an inefficient man, and an elusive one, for I
never met him then or afterwards.

Julian Symons was much the reverse. He not only liked to encourage young writers whom he felt had a flair for poetry; he liked
to encounter them and bring them together. It was almost a ritual procedure. One was invited to a pub near Victoria Station for
a few preliminary drinks and a looking over, and then to gatherings
where other poets appeared, sometimes in the Victoria pub, sometimes in the *Salisbury* on St. Martin's Lane, and sometimes at that
incredibly cheap and good Italian restaurant, *Poggioli's* in Charlotte
Street, where spaghetti could be had for sevenpence, a ravioli for
ninepence, and a *Chateaubriand garni* large enough for two people
to share for half a crown. It was at these gatherings that I began to
meet the late Thirties poets who were my contemporaries — Herbert
Mallalieu and Ruthven Todd, Keidrych Rhys and Derek Savage and
Philip O'Connor — and Roy Fuller.

At this time I was socially naive, trained to provincial plebeian
manners. As one did in my mainly telephoneless Shropshire small
town, I would call on people without notice, and it often needed
some heavy hints to get me leaving. Kathleen Raine, who observed

me with amusement while she endured me, said to me when we met again about eight years afterwards: "But how you've grown up! You were so *young* then!"

It was with typical gaucherie that, having met Roy Fuller twice in Julian's pub sessions, I wandered over to his maisonette, also in Blackheath, one day when I was staying with my aunt in a nearby suburb. I knocked on the door; Roy opened it, looking rather huffy at my intrusion, but asked me in, and immediately his wife Kate, that marvellously warm-hearted person, made me at home. Once the ice was thawed, everything went well, for we all came from above the Trent, that symbolic river which in England is held to divide the vigorous north-country people from the effete southerners.

I cannot have outstayed my welcome on that occasion, for I went several times to the maisonette before it was destroyed by a landmine during the blitz. Kate and their small son John (now the outstanding poet and critic John Fuller) went to Blackpool when the war began, but she ventured back to London occasionally, for I remember particularly one evening when she was there, and the sirens sounded; Roy and Kate would not let me out into the night, where shrapnel from the anti-aircraft shells was a greater danger even than the bombs, and I lay in their spare bedroom listening to the heavy thrum of the German planes, and the whistling sound of the bombs followed by their explosions, that night fortunately relatively remote.

In the spring of 1940, after *New Verse* and *Twentieth Century Verse* had expired as casualties of the war, I tried to make up for their absence by publishing a little magazine called *NOW*, which appeared intermittently between 1940 and 1947. Roy contributed to the first issue, and continued during the magazine's first two years — several of his poems appearing, as well as a story called "Fletcher" and, curiously, a note on Swinburne. I am sure he thought the anarchist slant of the journal more than a little dotty, for it would not be unfair to say that he was, then, a Communist fellow traveller, even a half-hearted apologist for Stalin, though this did not prevent his friendship with Julian Symons, then a Trotskyite, from continuing.

Roy went into the navy and went through the war perhaps not happily, but at least without seeing action. He spent a long time in poetically productive inactivity at various stations in Africa, and then returned with a commission to work in the Admiralty. Sometimes, impressive in his uniform, he would meet me — his conscientious objector friend then evading the authorities — for lunch at some discreet Soho haunt, like Mrs. Maurer's delicatessen on Dean Street or the Spanish restaurant run by the anarchist Pepe Pradas on Old

Compton Street.   Later Roy moved back to Blackheath and Kate and
Johnny joined him, living on the ground floor of a large Victorian
house; Julian and Kathleen Symons later moved into the top flat in
the same house, and Inge and I would pay joint visits to them fairly
often until we left for Canada in 1949, Roy and Julian both thinking
we were crazy to go, and Orwell only approving. (Roy, incidentally,
detested Orwell by repute, though he had never met him, while Julian and I became his close friends.) After our departure, we kept in
touch for forty years by correspondence, even occasional phone calls,
but I saw Roy only on my rare visits to England, though Julian has
twice travelled to Vancouver.

I suppose both Roy and I were nearer to Julian than we were to
each other; for, though the youngest of the three, he was by far the
most emphatic personality. We were all born in 1912 and within
less than four months of each other, Roy on the 18th February, I on
the 8th May and Julian on the 30th May. Other factors may have
drawn us together. We were all brought up, not without difficulty,
by mothers after our fathers had died during our childhood. Unlike
the elder poets of the Thirties (Spender only three years older but
a real generation gap between), we were not Oxbridge products, nor
indeed had we attended any university except for Roy's brief law
courses at London. And none of us belonged to what Julian called
the "homosexual sodality" which so dominated the orthodox avant-
gardism of the times.

Even the broadness of our scope as writers showed similarities.
Roy began as a poet, but quickly took up criticism, and after the war
fiction. Julian, beginning as a poet and editor, became not only a
notable critic, but also a celebrated detective story writer (a genre
in which Roy also wrote much). And I, also poet and editor for a
start, became a critic, a travel writer and a historian, though feats in
fiction, beyond short stories published at extraordinary intervals, are
yet in my eighties to come.

All of us, as well, have written autobiographically, and perhaps
it is here, in this shared field, that our differences of temperament,
experience, craft, have been most evident. Julian, in his *Notes from
Another Country*, and in the autobiographical essays in *Critical Observations* (one of which concerns his friendship with me), writes with
the irony and poise and extraordinary critical justice of one brought
up in a metropolitan literary background; his elder brother, after all,
was A.J.A. Symons, the highly original biographer of "Baron Corvo".
Julian's autobiographical approach is the facetted one; the memoir
seems to swing like some mirrored mobile, with each face showing a

different aspect of his life, his personal relations, and hence of him, but nothing in fact as highly structured as one of his novels; the self portrait is Protean, the panorama of the age is tentative.

Temperament as well as cultural background emerges in these matters, and in my own volumes of autobiography, *Letter to the Past* and *Beyond the Blue Mountain*, a certain Glendowerish quality emerges, a touch of Celtic afflatus proper to a Welsh Marcher, the desire to build a structured myth of a whole life, to find a pattern or a plot where plots can perhaps be held not to exist. For when we move on to Roy Fuller's autobiographical writings, collected in *The Strange and the Good*, it is clear that the importance of eloquence and the justification of dominant patterning and plot in memoirs can be debated and a different approach presented.

Towards the end of *Home and Dry*, the last part of *The Strange and the Good* — to discussing which I shall devote the rest of this essay — Roy offers some reflections on the nature of autobiography. I have always regarded both biography and autobiography, and indeed also any history that is more than mere factual chronicle, as by necessity forms of fiction, giving a shape that is the writer's intervention to the chaos of existence. But Roy makes a distinction between biography and autobiography, and one that causes one to reflect immediately on his own autobiographical achievement.

> Reading a biography, though carried along by the sequence, one may wonder what the plot is or is to be. The reflection must be followed immediately by the conclusion — a more or less obvious or banal one — that the point of every such work is the progress towards death. What a phenomenally prolonged preparation for the final few pages, the most compelling and moving! By comparison, an autobiography is plotless; in fact usually resembles the experimental novel (mentioned in *Souvenirs*) I conceived as an adolescent but fortunately made little progress with, a novel beginning normally but gradually getting more and more boring — for childhood has the plot of growing up as well as incidental freshness and sharpness, whereas (to bring in another art) adulthood is usually a mere, and more weakly orchestrated, recapitulation. However, the war, preceded by the threat of war, seems to me to have donated a further plot to the "growing-up" part of my life, and the *denouement* of that further plot — the coming of peace — is, of course, containable in autobiographical form, unlike death. (*The Strange and the Good*, 261)

One can readily grant Roy's remarks about biography; they explain the universal shallowness of Lives written while their subjects are still alive. The great shadow is then absent, and the account seems two-dimensional, unless the biography is of a person distinguished by a single, great and unrepeated achievement, when the plot may indeed close before death. Fuller is not denying the possibility of plot in autobiography, for he merely says that "By comparison" it is plotless, and then, in his own life, goes on to suggest the two plot cycles of childhood and later of involvement in a war. So here the author is giving us the criteria by which he would like us to judge his memoirs. They do not have the grandeur and tragedy of a *complete* Life, since they are not yet terminated by the end the writer cannot himself witness. On the other hand they are allowed, with seeming reluctance, to settle down into the unemphatically defined form of the three sections originally published as small books, *Souvenirs*, mainly about a Lancashire childhood and youth; *Vamp Till Ready*, mainly about coming out into the world, experiences as an apprentice lawyer, first months in the Royal Navy; and *Home and Dry*, telling of seasons in Africa (the farthest and most exotic travels of his life) and his last days of naval service in the limbo of the Admiralty.

I find *Souvenirs* the most compelling of all the three memoirs, even if too near the bone of my own childhood to be entirely conge-nial, because of the undramatic authenticity with which it describes a lower-middle-class north-country youth. Roy remarks that after his father's death "the petty bourgeois life — carless, servantless, seats in the pit rather than the dress circle — to which we were suddenly re-turned was far from uncongenial to me." (*The Strange and the Good*, 15) And he evokes remarkably the special kind of populated solitude endured by a semi-orphan child in such a setting, where the fellowship of the working class does not survive. At one point he remarks that "In literature truth about life cannot be attempted without truth about society, which is where much post-war fiction and drama is shaky, though the deficiency may be common in feebler writers in all epochs." (*The Strange and the Good*, 108–9) And one must say that his settings, his backgrounds, are vigorously populated, "my sense of the ludicrous in human character" (*The Strange and the Good*, 14) be-ing well displayed; they are also evocatively incidental. "The minutiae of life, often of what I have called the nose-picking variety. . .absorbed me," Roy remarks (*The Strange and the Good*, 143), and there are indeed times when one feels enough of the minutiae is enough, but other times when episodes glow, as they do again in the African pages of *Home and Dry*, with an immediate lambency of telling that does not diminish their completeness as memories.

Roy's earlier childhood setting was the Industrial Revolution town-scape of cotton-milling Oldham, which sheltered a way of life resembling that of Arnold Bennet's Five Towns, though less in speech than in social attitudes. While his father was alive the family enjoyed a modest prosperity and lived for a while in a largish house on the sooty rural verges of Oldham.

> The road the house was in led through the moorland to tiny grey-black manufacturing towns in the steep valleys, a landscape that still seems to me mysterious and haunting — just as the mill-dominated streets of urban east Lancashire, so long quitted, remain, as the phrase goes, my spiritual home. (*The Strange and the Good*, 12)

(Can here be a cause of Fuller's detestation of Orwell: that Orwell went to Wigan, a similar Lancashire town to Roy's "spiritual home", and came away with a dark image that missed all the human minutiae, the boyhood pleasures, that rooted Roy to this blasted landscape?)

The "mysterious and haunting" — how fleetingly it is mentioned, how scantily developed in Fuller's memoirs! There is much well observed and remembered of the daily details of lower-middle-class life in Oldham and the plebeian seaside resort of Blackpool to which Roy and his mother moved after his father's death. But there is equally well no effort to come to terms with those "mysterious and haunting" Pennine moorlands, to evoke them in the same way as other writers — Roy's near contemporaries — have done. There is none of the child's perceptive magic that one finds in Herbert Read's evocation of the Yorkshire dales and moors in *The Innocent Eye*. There is nothing either of that moving relation of the secret nature of the land and the secret nature of the soul which one finds in a Pennine poem like Auden's "In Praise of Limestone".

Fuller, as one recognizes from reading his poems and fiction as well as his autobiographies, was a writer for whom — except in the restricted and quasi-legal sense of solving a crime — mystery was not important, or perhaps rather, was not penetrable. He presented himself as — and by and large he has been — *l'homme moyen sensuel* (significantly professing atheism rather than agnosticism) to whom the surface of the earth was more important than its depths, and for whom the strange and wonderful become comprehensible when translated into familiar forms, even familiar conventions. I am thinking particularly of his reactions to darkest Africa, whose heart he had the good fortune to enter on a long trip to and around Lake Victoria Nyanza. He never tried to penetrate what mysteries might lie behind the visible facts; when he felt them hovering he put on a strange armour of associations derived from literature, evoking Conrad especially, Graham Greene occasionally, once even — albeit jestingly — Somerset Maugham.

And just as mystery is acknowledged but evaded, so the passionate — or at least the passionate expression — is avoided. With many writers one has to push aside the hyperbole of expression to get at the reality of an emotion. With Fuller one has to discount the modesty of utterance, or sometimes its mock-erudite complexity (what strange deposits have silted down from a long, assiduous reading of Henry James!) which disguises the depth of feeling. His devotion to his wife and son are as obvious in the text, especially at the times of parting, as one has known them to be in real life. Yet his expression of such feeling is quietly matter-of-fact, and when he talks of his friendships it is often the element of amusement that predominates rather than that of admiration, a fact that contributes to the sharp vividness of his vignettes of people remembered for their idiosyncrasies, though at times their names may be forgotten. But his accounts of political feelings are even more tepid; and, at the end of *The Strange and the Good*, the accounts of minor militancy in his twenties seem inconsequential, coming as they do from one who had climbed without great effort fairly high into the establishment, as director of a major building society, Governor of the BBC, Oxford Professor of Poetry in succession to W.H. Auden, and C.B.E., all of them honours perhaps deserved by his work as a poet, even if they bear an ambiguous relationship to his never wholly abandoned radicalism of thought.

Ultimately, of course, the test of literary memoirs is how far they illuminate the sources of the creative work to which they are — however much virtuosity they display — ultimately secondary. For all his variety of public positions, Roy never became a practically committed activist — radical or reactionary — but his very minor political role and his insecure convictions do have a bearing on our consideration of his poetry. Once he defined his role as the discovery of "private images of public ills", and his pleasure with minutiae, translated into verse, has resulted in a poetry that is concerned less with technical virtuosity (though Roy was never less than a superb and careful craftsman) than with the way in which the poet, never presented as more than an ordinary man, adjusts to the circumstances of society as he finds it and seeks to help alleviate its ills, but not without pessimism regarding human follies and faults. I remember once, some years ago, Roy addressing a questionnaire circulated by some little magazine, and answering the question: "Which animals do you prefer to man?" with the single word, "All".

The memoirs give us, in hindsight as it were, the minutiae of observation and experience (yes, often "nose-picking") that have been the
matter of his poetry, its basis and its expression. And they project
a matter-of-fact, man-of-letterish attitude to the act of writing. No
inspirational afflatus here! No romantic idea of the poet's role! (Roy
had little use for the bardic poetry and stance of Dylan Thomas and
dismissed him, like Orwell, as dotty.) Nor is there a suspicion of the
kind of inflationary currency offered by the teachers of "creative writing" in his talking about getting down to the poetic work, and his
counsel to apprentice writers:

> It is the only advice one can give to the young; work regularly; rewrite;
> keep a journal, a commonplace book, indulge yourself with pens, note-
> book, paper, typewriter, for they will inspire when life has failed. (*The
> Strange and the Good*, 57)

And here we are approaching the one mystery that Roy Fuller faced
and engaged, the mystery of literary creation, that underworld of
spells and talismans and never-ending practice, out of which the art
of poetry emerges; and engaged with continuing skill and intensity of
expression during that long career, from the time at which he began
to write in the nineteen-twenties and to publish in the early nineteen-
thirties, two thirds of a century ago.

The memoirs are, in fact, almost a model account of how a poet
in our age relates to and derives from his setting, and how that setting both shelters and nourishes him. For in spite of all that Fuller
may have had to say about the act of writing, the habit is no more
necessary than the habitat.

Note

Quotations are from *The Strange and the Good: Collected Memoirs* by Roy
Fuller (London: Collins-Harvill, 1991).

STEPHEN SPENDER

Two Worlds

Roy Fuller was one of the most important English poets of our time, with a very distinct individual voice and beautiful command of form. His poems often strike me as being muted autobiography; and, running parallel with the poetry, are four volumes of memoirs: *Souvenirs* (1980); *Vamp Till Ready* (1982); *Home and Dry* (1984); and *Spanner and Pen* (1990).

Several themes run through these memoirs: one, the deepest, like a subterranean stream out of which the others proceed, is that of Fuller's provincial small town origins, contrasted implicitly with the Oxford/Cambridge/London background of his near contemporaries, the Thirties poets — Auden, Day Lewis, etc. — whose early success was helped by their privileged status.

A slight feeling of the writer having "chips" is more an advantage than the reverse. It acts as some piquant sauce sharpening the account of life as a solicitor within the Woolwich Equitable Building Society that he gives in his fourth volume, *Spanner and Pen*. There is something here of the early H.G. Wells of *Kipps*. And, if the climate is Wellsian, Fuller also has a Chekhovian gift for creating vignettes of several characters encountered in his varied career.

A second theme, in his last volume, was his unashamed success in scaling the ladders of two quite separate careers: one, as the Insurance Solicitor, the other as a poet in the perhaps narrower world of literary advancement. I should add to this a third theme, implicit throughout: that, for him, it was the poetry, not the reputation, that counted.

Sometimes the high rungs of achievement on the one ladder promote advancement on the other. Thus his distinction at the Company Board Meeting of the "Woolwich" may have been a recommendation to his position as a governor of the B.B.C. — described by him as most enjoyable. On the other hand, when, as poet, he was appointed Chairman of the Literary Panel of the Arts Council, some of his writer colleagues — epitomised as "unregenerate lefties" — seemed to have been dismayed by the insuring side of a poet who for the most prudential reasons opposed zany projects funded under the heading "Performance Art". This makes painfully comic — or comically painful — reading.

In his memoirs, Roy Fuller describes his career as a published poet, much of it sad, though some editors (notably John Lehmann) from the first to last supported him. One has the feeling here that the many honours and distinctions he received, wholly deserved as they were, shed an ironic light on the early neglect of that for which he most sought recognition, his poetry.

His books are more than literary biography. They illuminate two worlds — the institutional and the literary life of the country. The way in which he made himself at home in both of them is very reassuringly English.

PETER READING

For Roy Fuller

53 bus approaching the terminus;
  dapper sartorial English elder
  suited in Manx tweed, close-clipped grey tash:

Too much is wrong, Gibbonian undertones,
  schooling and bread and dress and manners,
era's decline, Elgarian sadnesses;
too much is wrong, duff ticker, insomnia,
  ulcer and thyrotoxicosis,
    end of the world in one's lifetime likely,
flight of a sparrow brief through the feasting hall.

GEORGE JOHNSTON

A Lament for Roy Fuller
and gratitude for *Available for Dreams*

At close of day comes clink of ice in glass;
Awaited chime that, cares of day dispersed,
Beckons the poet to a grateful thirst
And brief dismissal of the world. Alas
That the world dismisses us. As the grass
The Good Book says all flesh is, and our nursed
Dram is a fleeting gesture at the Worst,
Slunk to his corner for our sweet recess.

Suddenly we are old, and our bones ache
According to what tune the weather plays;
And our hearts ache, as they have done and done
Whether in God's blessing or the warm sun.
Now you have drifted from our world of days,
But not your poems. We thank you for their sake.

JULIAN SYMONS

The Enterprise of St Mary's Bay

In the late summer of 1936 I sent out something like a thousand circulars announcing the birth of a magazine, *Twentieth Century Verse*, in the expectation that I should get two hundred subscriptions. I say "something like" because I received only nine subscriptions, and it's very possible that after sending out with so little result several hundred of these single sheets which said the magazine was "not committed to the support of any artistic clique or political party" but would be published "for that part of the civilised minority interested in the development of verse to-day" I gave up the attempt to get advance subscriptions. At the bottom of the circular was the usual tear-off strip, and one of the nine returned came from R.B. Fuller at an address in Kennington, Ashford, Kent, name and address written in a neat clerkly hand, the four shilling subscription enclosed. An absurdly small amount, it may seem, but the production cost of printing a thousand copies of the magazine was never more than 15 pounds.

Small insoluble mysteries occur to me with that first paragraph set down. Where did I get the addresses to send circulars, and in particular Fuller's address? More than half a century later I can't remember. His name was known to me as a contributor elsewhere, in particular to Roger Roughton's *Contemporary Poetry and Prose*, and with my own first issue out I invited him to submit poems. A reply said that "most of my recent verse is under consideration by an American periodical" but two poems came, both of which I printed. One was a sestina rather distinctly after Auden, the other a memorable short poem beginning "In the morning I visited her again, she lay/O horror! bloodless and the curtains flapping". A month later he submitted five poems, of which I think I printed two, and after that he was one of the magazine's most regular contributors during its three years' life.

When did we first meet? Not for several months certainly, perhaps not until early in 1938. He, for some reason perhaps associated with that phrase invoking the "civilised minority", had an image of a "wispy figure more like an ineffectual Nineties poet than someone able to stand up to the rigours of the Thirties." He was surprised to meet what his memoirs call a tough-minded six footer, "notable eater

and drinker, expert table tennis and snooker player". I had no particular preconception about Roy's appearance and attitudes, although
he had written to me: "God knows, I am the most orthodox Marxist"
in the course of telling me that he had never received any notice from
Left Review. I was at that time a very unorthodox Marxist, perhaps
not yet the card-carrying member of the Fourth International I briefly
became, but unlikely to be favourably inclined towards a committed
CP member. The person I met, however, was a handsome slim figure of medium height, soberly dressed yet giving a slightly dandyish
impression, with a pleasant voice that retained a slight trace of Lancastrian origin, and a manner originally cautious but within a few
minutes easy, down-to-earth, at times sharp or ironic. I took him,
not to the good restaurant he may have been expecting (he may have
nursed the illusion before meeting me that I was a man with a private
income rather than a wage slave), but to the excellent Tichelaars in
Wilton Road, where one could get a dozen portuguese oysters for two
shillings and much robust food of a generally Germanic kind. Roy's
digestion was at that time in good order, and although I can't remember what we ate it may well have been the fattish belly of pork he
often ordered later on when we ate at Schmidt's in Charlotte Street.

So at this first meeting we knew and liked each other. It was
succeeded by evenings in pubs where I occasionally summoned contributors to discuss the fate of poetry in the Thirties, and at a party in
my basement Pimlico flat. There were areas where we trod delicately,
not only those political ones in which I thought him hopelessly naive
and he found me foolishly romantic. What he calls in his memoirs
"the parrot and jackdaw ways" of my friend Ruthven Todd "used
to offend (his) Lancastrian puritanism", and at the time this was
a feeling I respected but didn't share. I remember taking him one
evening for drinks and chat at the Soho flat of the Surrealist artist
Toni del Renzio. There he sat completely silent for a couple of hours
in the midst of what I suppose was distastefully bohemian talk, until
I took mercy on him and said we must go. Why didn't he just get
up and leave? That might have hurt my feelings and Roy, although
then capable of off hand rudeness on occasion, always respected the
susceptibilities of anybody he liked.

Looking at my incomplete file of our correspondence I see with
surprise that we remained on surname terms until mid-1938 — until,
in fact, I suggested we might go on holiday together, along with my
friends Herbert and Marjorie Mallalieu. I suppose the basic reason for
the suggestion was that Fullers and Mallalieus both had small sons
of approximately the same age, John Fuller being almost eighteen

months, Paul Mallalieu a couple of weeks younger. Even so, as I look back I am astonished by my temerity. I had never met Roy's wife Kate, and the Fullers did not know the Mallalieus. More surprising still, in view of the characteristic Fuller caution, is Roy's easy acceptance of the suggestion. "We hadn't arranged to go anywhere — your suggestion is most apt and welcome", he wrote. "A village on the coast would be the thing, if such exists within reasonable reach. But perhaps any questions are premature — the point is we should like very much to go with you." His next letter revealed his first Christian name, which apparently I hadn't known, adding that the second (Broadbent) was "a family name, repellent and barbaric, and best left in the shadows." It must have been soon afterwards that, ignoring W.H. Auden and W.B. Yeats, I blithely told him that initials were no good for a poet, a Christian name was vital, and R.B. became Roy Fuller on the printed page.

But where to go? Devon was thought too far and, Roy said, "a long train journey with infants comes straight out of Dante". I consulted *Dalton's Weekly*, where I had found the Pimlico flat in which I was living, and other suggestions were made. Suffolk? "It sounds flat and bleak and full of chapped girls slitting herrings". What about the Golf House, St Margarets-at-Cliff, in Kent, 3 beds, bathroom, 2 rec rooms, garden 1/2 acre, summer 2/5 guineas"? This was Roy's discovery, and I can't think why we didn't take it. We eventually settled on a bungalow at St Mary's Bay, on the Kent coast between Dymchurch and Hythe, which I found in *Dalton's*. It cost 6 guineas, whether per week or for the two weeks of our stay I'm not sure. Roy wrote: "My wife, having through long contact with me acquired something of my cautious legal mind, tells me to warn you that St Mary's Bay is bleak, flat and unromantic: we thus avoid any responsibility for Mallalieu putting his head in the cook-an-heat (sic) after a couple of days." I am giving only a fragment of a correspondence which moved away from places to rent to chat about poems, novels ("We all ought to write novels. In fact we all ought to give up our jobs and live at the Old Golf House") and politics ("Edmund Wilson is no friend of the working class under any banner," Roy wrote after reading the Trotskyist *Partisan Review*. "I wish you were an orthodox Marxist so that you could run a red monthly on the reasonable middle line.")

St Mary's Bay was easily reached from the Fuller's home outside Ashford, and the journey from the Mallalieus' Croydon maisonette was not difficult. On a Saturday — lettings of such places were, and are, from Saturday to Saturday — I went down to Ashford, was greeted by Roy wearing very natty red braces, and met Kate for the first time. I admired her neatness, stylishness, efficiency, lack of fuss. In no time she had cooked lunch, washed it up with our help, and we were off. We took first an orthodox train, then one of the tiny carriages on the Romney, Hythe and Dymchurch Railway, which stopped at St Mary's Bay. From the station we walked to the bungalow, Kate or Roy pushing John. Within an hour or two the Mallalieus joined us, along with Paul.

I had known Herbert and Marjorie Mallalieu longer, and much better, than I knew Roy. *Twentieth Century Verse* had been hatched in their Croydon home where I lived for a year. They helped send out the circulars, and later on Herbert in one fine spurt of energy obtained several advertisements for the magazine from publishers. Such frenetic but short-lived enthusiasm was typical of Herbert. "Darkly handsome" is the phrase used about him by Roy in his memoirs, to which I should have added that he had great charm. He was quick-minded and had a passionate feeling for poetry — at this time for Percy's Reliques and the Border Ballads, Hopkins and Eliot and the minor Elizabethans. In the affairs of life, however, Herbert was butterfly-minded, full of schemes for running a magazine, becoming an actor, making money, which came to nothing. He had been a journalist on a Croydon paper and the *Sunday Referee*, was diagnosed as tubercular, spent three months in a hospital, discharged himself, and took an African witch-doctor's recipe called Umckaloabo which cured him. His wife Marjorie was, like him, enthusiastic, volatile, bohemian in not being too greatly concerned about money or the lack of it. Few couples could have differed more in behaviour and attitudes to life than the Mallalieus and the Fullers. At the time it did not occur to me that this might cause problems, and if I had thought of the possibility I should probably have ignored it.

And in fact we all got on very well, or at least that's the way I remember it, the nearest approach to a sense of strain coming through my forgetfulness. Marjorie Mallalieu was working, and a girl named Agnes looked after Paul. Agnes came with them on holiday, and they assumed she would look after the children, with the Fullers paying half her wages. I'd forgotten to mention this to the Fullers, and Kate had no intention of letting somebody else look after her child, particularly perhaps because Paul showed a distinct tendency to claim possession of spades, buckets and toys, and do battle if this was disputed by John.

This and one or two other trivialities apart, there were no problems. I remember the weather as continuously good, although that is probably an illusion. Certainly we swam a lot, played games on the beach, wrote poems, did some moderate pub drinking in the evenings, not much disturbed by the fact that St Mary's Bay was no better than Kate's description of it. One incident established Roy permanently in my mind as possessing miraculous powers of observation. As a result of boxing without a gum shield in adolescence I had loosened two front teeth, which eventually had to be replaced by a small plate. When swallowing a mouthful of sea water I coughed, expelled the plate, and emerged horribly gap-toothed. Ducking and diving under water proved useless. A few hours later, the tide out, we wandered, hopelessly as I felt, about the stony beach looking for the tiny plate. But — I can hardly believe it even now — after a few minutes Roy gave a cry, and held up the sea-washed teeth.

How did we spend our time? In his memoirs Roy mentions arduous evenings of paper games. Certainly Herbert and I were devoted to them (when I lived at Croydon we spent whole evenings playing a cricket game called Stumpz), and Roy was not disinclined, Marjorie and Kate perhaps pressed into playing. We also read poetry aloud, talked about current poetry and poets, argued about politics, discussed cricket prospects, played a sort of tennis quoits in the garden. The owner of the bungalow, whose name was Cooper, lived locally and we detected him snooping around, or at least thought he was doing so. He complained afterwards that we had caused some damage, probably in the form of cigarette burns, Fullers and Mallalieus then being steady smokers. Roy wrote to me afterwards, saying Cooper had been seen snooping in Ashford and adding, not seriously: "We make it clear that personally we deny liability." At the end of two weeks we had all run out of money. On our last day I remember Kate making a delicious onion tart, onions and flour the only things left.

Fullers and Mallalieus saw each other only occasionally after the enterprise of St Mary's Bay, but for me it was the start of a lifelong friendship. In the Fullers' Blackheath flat I met Kathleen Clark whom I married, we saw Roy often in the early part of the war and when he returned from Africa, and after the war ended Kathleen and I lived for five years on the top floor of a big Victorian house in Blackheath, the Fullers on the ground floor. Football became something like an obsession, and in those years we went to almost every Charlton home match. Kate drove me to the ground once in the Fullers' very first car — a car was something none of us aspired to before the war — and thought mistakenly that her driving would make me nervous. The acquisition of cars (Kathleen and I bought one rather later, in 1950) marks in a small way the difference between our pre- and post-war lives, so that the carless pleasures of St Mary's Bay could never have been repeated. That pre-war holiday remains vivid in my mind, an image of the days when all of us lived what seem now uncomplicated and even innocent lives, our beliefs and hopes preserving us from some of the nastier realities of the world around us.

ANTHONY THWAITE

After the Japanese
(For Roy)

If only, when the news came through
Old Age was on the way,
One shut the door, said 'Not at home',
And turned the bore away.

*

Though we had always known it was the way
We had to follow at the very end,
We never thought as yesterday went by
That it would be the road we walk today.

APPENDIX

A Bibliography of Books by Roy Fuller

(Compiled by A.T. Tolley)

Poetry

Poems (London: Fortune, 1939)

The Middle of a War (London: Hogarth Press, 1942)

A Lost Season (London: Hogarth Press, 1944)

Epitaphs and Occasions (London: Lehmann, 1949)

Counterparts (London: Verschoyle, 1954)

Brutus's Orchard (London: Deutsch 1957; New York, Macmillan, 1958)

Collected Poems 1936 – 1961 (London: Deutsch, 1962; Philadelphia: Dufour, 1962)

Spring Song (Colchester: Colchester School of Art, 1963)

Buff (London: Deutsch, 1965; Chester Springs, Pa.: Dufour, 1965)

Confrontation Off Korea (Oxford: Sycamore, 1968)

New Poems (London: Deutsch, 1968; Chester Springs, Pa.: Dufour, 1968)

Pergamon Poets I: Roy Fuller and R.S. Thomas (London: Pergamon, 1968)

Off Course (London: Turret Books, 1969)

Penguin Modern Poets 18 (with Alfred Alvarez & Anthony Thwaite) (Harmondsworth: Penguin, 1970)

To an Unknown Reader (London: Poem-of-the-Month Club, 1970)

Song Cycle for a Record Sleeve (Oxford: Sycamore Press, 1972)

The CCC (Privately printed, 1972)

Tiny Tears (London: Deutsch, 1973)

Cars in a Life (Kettering: Carroll, 1974)

An Old War (Edinburgh: Tragara, 1974)

Waiting for the Barbarians (Richmond, Surrey: The Keepsake Press, 1974)

From the Joke Shop (London: Deutsch, 1975)

The Joke Shop Annexe (Edinburgh: Tragara, 1975)

An Ill-Governed Coast (Sunderland: Ceolfrith, 1976)

The Souvenirs of S.O.G. (Privately printed, 1977)

Pictures of a Winter (Colchester: Colchester School of Art, 1978)

Re-Treads (Edinburgh: Tragara, 1979)

Notebook (Taurus Press of the Willow Dene, 1979)

Swann on the Isis (Privately printed, 1979)

The Reign of Sparrows (London: London Magazine Editions, 1980)

More About Tompkins (Edinburgh: Tragara, 1981)

House and Shop (Edinburgh: Tragara, 1982)

The Individual and His Times: a selection of the poetry of Roy Fuller, ed. V.J. Lee (London: Athlone Press, 1982)

As from the Thirties (Edinburgh: Tragara, 1983)

Howard Castled (Privately printed, 1983)

Mianserin Sonnets (Edinburgh: Tragara, 1984)

New and Collected Poems 1934-1984 (London: Secker and Warburg in association with London Magazine Editions, 1985)

Subsequent to Summer (Edinburgh: Salamander Press, 1985)

Iron Aspidistra (as by "Mark Members") (Oxford: Sycamore Press, 1985)

Outside the Canon (Edinburgh: Tragara, 1986)

Consolations (London: Secker and Warburg, 1987)

Lessons of the Summer (Edinburgh: Tragara, 1987)

Available for Dreams (London: Collins Harvill, 1989)

Verse for Children

Seen Grandpa Lately (London: Deutsch, 1972)

Poor Roy (London: Deutsch, 1977)

Upright Downfall (with Barbara Giles & Adrian Rumble) (London: Oxford, 1983)

The World Through the Window: Collected Poems for Children (London: Blackie, 1989)

Novels

Image of a Society (London: Deutsch, 1956; New York: Macmillan, 1957)

The Ruined Boys (London: Deutsch, 1959; (as *That Distant Afternoon*) New York: Macmillan, 1959)

The Father's Comedy (London: Deutsch, 1961)

The Perfect Fool (London: Deutsch, 1961)

My Child, My Sister (London: Deutsch, 1965)

The Carnal Island (London: Deutsch, 1970)

Stares (London: Sinclair-Stevenson, 1990)

Fables

The Other Planet (Richmond, Surrey: The Keepsake Press, 1979)

Crime Novels

With My Little Eye (London: Lehmann, 1948; New York: Macmillan, 1957)

The Second Curtain (London: Verschoyle, 1953; New York: Macmillan, 1956)

Fantasy and Fugue (London: Verschoyle, 1954; New York: Macmillan, 1956; (as *Murder in Mind*) Chicago: Academy, 1986)

Crime Omnibus (*With My Little Eye*; *The Second Curtain*; *Fantasy and Fugue*) (Manchester: Carcanet, 1988)

Fiction for Children

Savage Gold (London: Lehmann, 1946)

Catspaw (London: Ross, 1966)

Autobiography

Souvenirs (London: London Magazine Editions, 1980)

Vamp Till Ready (London: London Magazine Editions, 1982)

Home and Dry (London: London Magazine Editions, 1984)

The Strange and the Good: Collected Memoirs (shortened version of *Souvenirs*; *Vamp Till Ready*; *Home and Dry*) (London: Collins-Harvill, 1989)

Spanner and Pen (London: Sinclair-Stevenson, 1991)

Criticism

Owls and Artificers (London: Deutsch, 1971; New York: Library Press, 1971)

Professors and Gods (London: Deutsch, 1973; New York: St. Martin's Press, 1974)

Twelfth Night: a personal view (Edinburgh: Tragara, 1985)

Other Non-Fiction

Questions and Answers in Building Society Law and Practice (London: Franey, 1949)

Edited by Roy Fuller

The Confidence Man by Herman Melville, with Introduction by Roy Fuller (London: Lehmann, 1948)

Byron for Today, selected with an Introduction by Roy Fuller (London: Porcupine, 1949)

New Poems 1952. Edited by Roy Fuller, Clifford Dyment & Montague Slater (London: Michael Joseph, 1952)

The Building Societies Act, 1874 – 1960, Great Britain and Northern Ireland, with extracts from associated legislation
(4th edition) ed. R.B. Fuller (London: Franey, 1959)
(5th edition) (London: Franey, 1961)
(6th edition) (London: Franey, 1962)

Supplement to New Poetry (London: Poetry Book Society, 1964)

Fellow Mortals: an Anthology of Animal Verse (Plymouth: Macdonald & Evans, 1981)

The Penguin New Writing: 1940 – 1950 (with John Lehmann) (Harmondsworth: Penguin, 1985)

Notes on Contributors

ALLAN AUSTIN is a professor at the University of Guelph and author of *Roy Fuller*, published by Twayne.

JONATHAN BARKER is with the British Council. He has written extensively about modern British poetry. He has recently co-edited *Collected Poems and Selected Translations* of Norman Cameron for Anvil Press.

BERNARD BERGONZI is Professor Emeritus of the University of Warwick. His books include *Heroes' Twilight*, *The Situation of the Novel* and *Exploding English*.

ALAN BROWNJOHN is a poet whose *Collected Poems* were published in 1983 and 1988. His first novel, *The Way You Tell Them*, appeared in 1990.

GAVIN EWART is a poet and lifelong admirer of Roy Fuller.

JOHN FULLER is a fellow of Magdalen College, Oxford and son of Roy Fuller. His novel, *Flying to Nowhere*, won the Whitbread Prize. His latest novel is *Look Twice*. He has published several volumes of poetry.

BARBARA GABRIEL is a professor at Carleton University in Ottawa.

GEORGE JOHNSTON is a poet and Professor Emeritus of Carleton University.

CHRISTOPHER LEVENSON, co-founder and former editor of *Arc*, is a poet whose latest book, *Duplicities: New and Selected Poems*, appeared in 1992.

PETER LEVI is a poet and former Professor of Poetry at Oxford. His lectures appeared as *The Art of Poetry* in 1991.

NEIL POWELL is a poet who was early encouraged by Roy Fuller. His recent books include *True Colours* and a novel, *Unreal City*. He is writing an authorised critical biography of Roy Fuller.

PETER READING is a poet whose books include *Diplopic* and *C*.

SIR STEPHEN SPENDER is a poet and long-time friend of Roy Fuller.

DONALD STANFORD is a former editor of *Southern Review*, where he published work by Roy Fuller. Among his books are *In the Classic Mode* and *The Achievement of Robert Frost*.

JULIAN SYMONS is a critic, novelist and poet, and a lifelong friend of Roy Fuller. He published Fuller's earliest work in *Twentieth Century Verse* in the late thirties.

ANTHONY THWAITE is a poet and former editor of *Encounter*. His books include *A Portion for Foxes*, *Victorian Voices* and *Poems 1953–1988*. He has edited Philip Larkin's *Selected Letters*.

A.T. TOLLEY is the author of *The Poetry of the Thirties* and *The Poetry of the Forties*.

GEORGE WOODCOCK is a poet and critic and was editor of *Now* in the forties, where he published work by Roy Fuller. He was a lifelong friend of Fuller.